DEER HUNTER'S DEVOTIONAL

Also by Sean Jeffries

Eight Days in Africa – The Story of an African Safari

A Life Spent Afield
Short Essays on Hunting, Fishing, and the Sportsman's Way of Life

DEER HUNTER'S DEVOTIONAL
Hunting for the Heart of God

SEAN JEFFRIES

A *Wingshooters.net* Book

Clover, SC

Published in Clover, SC by Wingshooters.net

Scripture quotations taken from the New American Standard Bible®, Copyright © 1960, 1962, 1963, 1968, 1971, 1972, 1973, 1975, 1977, 1995 by The Lockman Foundation Used by permission. (www.Lockman.org)

Cover Photo copyright © 2010 by Todd Carlson. Used by permission.

Jeffries, Sean.
  Deer hunter's devotional: hunting for the heart of god / Sean Jeffries.

ISBN 10: 1-4537-5850-X (softcover)
ISBN 13: 978-1-4537-5850-2 (softcover)

Printed in the United States of America
10 9 8 7 6 5 4 3 2 1
FIRST EDITION

For my hunting buddies
Ted, Arnold, Pete, and the guys at the Liberty Hill lease.

Shoot straight, boys.

Contents

Free yourself, like a gazelle from the hand of the hunter,
Like a bird from the snare of the fowler.

Proverbs 6:5
World English Bible

AUTHOR'S NOTE

I'm aware that there are a few other devotionals on the market that are geared towards sportsmen. I've intentionally refrained from reading any of them in order to be sure to keep all of my material original. To the authors of those books, if we cross paths somewhere along the way in our works, I apologize for hunting in your territory, but it was completely accidental.

When I subtitled this book *"Hunting for the Heart of God,"* I had a larger purpose in mind than just having a catchy phrase that linked hunting and God together. I have a vision of a greater series of works that will fall under this same subtitle, ranging from this devotional to a collection of short essays, and ultimately to a novel that I am working on that goes under the temporary title of "Thursdays at the Cabin."

I'd like to see a movement towards Christ among sportsmen. For several years I've felt that call upon my life, and the time has come to take the first step toward making that happen. This book is designed to cause you to think about God when you step into the woods. I hope that in some small way I accomplished that.

As usual, a few thanks are in order. This time around, I'd like to thank my buddy Pete for proofing the manuscript. Thanks also to Matt Brinton for doing the same. The guys in my Band of Brothers were faithful in providing prayer cover as I wrote this book. I came under spiritual attack pretty heavily as I worked to get this done, and I appreciate the covering fire that they gave me. Frank, Pete, Stephen, and Travis: thanks.

Finally, thanks go to Todd Carlson for allowing me the use of his picture of "Big Bux" on the front cover. Todd has shared pictures of this majestic whitetail for many years on Ted Nugent's internet forum, and we've all enjoyed watching his incredible antlers grow.

Deer Hunter's Devotional

READING THIS DEVOTIONAL

Before we get into the text, I thought I'd take a minute to talk about how this book is laid out, and how it's designed to be read. Each chapter in it is written so that you can read it in a single sitting. Most of the chapters are only two or three pages in length, with an occasional entry going into a fourth or fifth page. I wanted to make sure that you could do your daily reading quickly while still giving you something that would, hopefully, be deep enough to provoke you to think about what you've read.

At the beginning of each chapter you'll find a verse of Scripture. I want to be clear on one thing here. The Bible has very few verses that directly refer to hunting. It's very easy to take a single verse out of context and make it mean anything that you want it to, and I have been very careful to avoid doing that. Each verse was prayerfully and carefully chosen, and the text that follows each one tries to keep close to the theme of the original context of that verse while still bringing hunting and the outdoors to mind.

This is not an expository book; that is, it does not try to explain each verse, but rather it uses each verse to set the tone for the text that follows. With that in mind, I encourage you to go back to your Bible and read each verse in its proper context and through this gain more familiarity with God's Word. Verses from a wide variety of books have been chosen to head each chapter.

Finally, at the end of each day's reading is an Action Point. The goal of these is to give you a clear target to shoot for both in the deer woods and in your walk with God. Each one is also designed to very briefly summarize the full text of each chapter. I've again put careful thought into each of these summaries, and hope that they are useful to you.

HUNTING FOR THE HEART OF GOD

"Then I will give you shepherds after My own heart, who will feed you on knowledge and understanding."

Jeremiah 3:15

I like to think about a lot of different things in the quiet stillness of a pre-dawn morning as I wait for the sun to rise in the deer woods. I find that once I get settled into my stand, my mind will often drift from one thought to another, but the topic that I land on the most often is my relationship with Christ. In a deer stand I'm able to do my most serious business with Him in those tranquil moments of the morning.

As I get older, it seems that my life has gotten far busier than I ever remember it being in my twenties and thirties. Over the last year or so, I've had to work much longer hours than ever before at my computer programming job; an eight hour day is a rarity for me, and I seldom seem to have an opportunity to just sit back and enjoy some quiet time. I can count the days that I've been able to simply relax after work in the last three months on the fingers of one hand.

Having a child on the way doesn't help things; it seems like there is something that has to be done every single day just to get ready for his birth. Whether we're out shopping for things for the nursery or going to the next doctor's appointment, it just seems like we're always in a rush. My wife and I are both greatly anticipating the arrival of our child, but I just didn't think that things would get this busy so quickly. It was my thinking that we'd be at our busiest *after* his birth, but I've found the opposite to be true.

When deer season finally comes around, I usually take every chance I get to go hunting simply because it gives me an opportunity to process all of the things that are on my mind. Being in a treestand forces me to be still and silent. While my eyes are alert for the flicker of a tail or the twitch of an ear, my mind is hard at work thinking about the things that I've stored up since the last time that I had a chance to spend a few hours alone. As this year's season comes around, I'll enter the woods with a new fervor as the goal of my hunting shifts away from deer and more toward God.

Over the last ten years alone, I've killed over forty deer. I've proven to myself that I have the ability to get out in the woods and get at least three deer per season, and it is no longer about the number of deer that I get. I've matured as a hunter, and am to the point where I simply sit back and watch the deer more often than I actually pull the trigger on one. I still hunt hard at the beginning of the year, wanting to be sure to put at least a little bit of venison in the freezer, but I feel like I'm much farther along in my hunting career than I was even five years ago.

My spiritual life has also been growing in many ways in the past few years. My buddy Frank and I have been meeting on a weekly basis to encourage each other in our Christian walks, and a group of three or four other men are joining us every few weeks as we start to "live in community", sharing our lives and our wounds, and teaching each other how to live as men of strength and honor. All of us are increasing in our knowledge of Christ and are seeing the fruit of this in our marriages and in our families.

I've begun to be more open in talking about Christ when I am with nonbelievers, and the focus of my writing has shifted more toward Him and farther away from simply telling hunting stories. I'm approaching spiritual warfare from a much more informed perspective, and I feel like my prayers are becoming more effective and focused.

If there's one place in my life that needs work though, it's my relationship with Christ at the deepest level; at the level of what author John Eldredge calls "conversational intimacy." That's one of the things that I hope to recover as I spend time afield during the deer season this year. I want to ratchet my prayer life up a notch; to speak with Christ as both King and Savior, to know Him as I never have before.

As I approach fatherhood, I want to know God as a Father even as I am asking Him to teach me to father my own child. I want to learn to trust God the way a child trusts his father. Although I know in my head that His will for me is perfect, I want to know this also in my heart. I'll spend a great deal of time in the woods this year thinking about this very thing.

While I'm afield this year, I'll certainly be hoping to bring home a few deer for the freezer, and maybe even a trophy buck for the living room wall. I'm planning on spending as much time as possible in the deer stand this season, and in my early scouting I've been seeing a lot of good deer sign. The trees are full of acorns, and the deer are plentiful. I can't wait for opening day. But this time around it's not really deer that I'm hunting for; it's the heart of God.

ACTION POINT: Think about what it is that you're really hunting for when you're in the woods this year. Is it just bigger antlers or more venison for the freezer, or are you looking for something much greater than that? Discover what "Hunting for the Heart of God" means in your own life.

CREATED IN THE WILDERNESS

"The LORD God planted a garden toward the east, in Eden; and there He placed the man whom He had formed."

Genesis 2:8

There is an excitement that stirs within me every time I enter the wilderness that is simply not present when I am in an urban or even a suburban environment. I am drawn to the wild places of the world; this yearning inside of me has taken me from the fields and woods of South Carolina to the barren mountains of southeastern Montana, and even far across the sea to the African bush. This excitement is the reason that I feel so much more alive when I am far from people and crowds.

I am extremely uncomfortable in large cities and in the modern high density neighborhoods. The first house that my wife and I bought was in this kind of neighborhood in Charlotte, North Carolina when we first got married. Our little house sat on less than a quarter of an acre of land, and I could not step outside onto the back deck without wondering if my neighbors could hear every word that I was saying. Drug dealers and signs of gang activity were becoming common in our area, and I once found the screen of our side window pried off where someone had attempted to break in while we were away. I moved us away from that wretched situation as quickly as I could, and I have never looked back. Getting me and my wife out of that situation was critical.

Some people are drawn to the lights and buildings of the city; to the crowds and restaurants and bars. These things are not for me. My heart leaps at the sight of a field of golden wheat, or a meadow of tall grass dotted with sprigs of dog fennel, or the marshes of the lowcountry. I was made for the wilderness, and I enter it as often as I am able. I love dirt roads, rivers, and hidden creeks in the depths of the forest. I yearn for the sight of tall oak trees and pines waving in the wind.

This passion for the outdoors is felt by a great many men, and I believe that it was set within us by God Himself. If you carefully read Genesis, you'll see that Adam was created outside of the Garden of Eden; he was only placed there *after* being formed from the dust of the earth. Not all men seem to hear this call; some people are extremely uncomfortable being in the wilds, but I believe that many men would jump at the chance for the adventures that the outdoor life offers.

I've often wondered what it is that draws some of us to those wild places, while others are extremely reluctant to go afield. It's more than an aversion to killing game; some men simply can't stand to be in the woods. It may be that these men simply weren't exposed to the outdoors as children, and thus are uncomfortable in an unfamiliar environment. For this reason I think it's important that we get our children outdoors at as early an age as possible.

In reading through Scripture, we often see where the great men of the Bible spent time in the wilderness. John the Baptist lived in the wilds, and his followers – some of whom became the Apostles of Christ – would have been out there with him. Jesus Himself often retreated to the mountains to pray, and He was taken to the wilderness to be tempted by Satan.

When Paul was on the road to Damascus, Christ appeared to him and asked him why he was persecuting the Son of God. Paul was, as you know, blinded during this event, and had to go to the house of Ananias where his vision was restored. One of the things that we often miss is that between the time that he regained his sight and the beginning of his ministry, he spent three years in the wilderness of Arabia receiving instructions from Christ.

Time and time again, events like this occur in the lives of our Biblical heroes. David hid from Saul in the desert, and Moses fled to Midian where he spent forty years of his life. God sends Abraham to the mountains to sacrifice his son Isaac. It happens over and over. If God used time in the wilderness to teach the men of the Bible about Him, then we too should try to discern what it is that He is teaching us when we are afield.

It's my firm belief that the reason that these men found God in the wild was that it was in those places of silence and solitude that they were able to fully focus on Him. If there was so much noise in the lives of these Biblical men that they had to go out into the wild to find God, how much more do we need similar time like this today, when our lives are constantly being bombarded with information overload?

If God is indeed trying to teach me something when I am hunting and fishing, then it's up to me to seek His heart and face during my time in the woods. God is speaking to us through His creation; it's vital that we listen to what He is saying and apply the lessons that we learn to our lives both in and out of the wilderness.

ACTION POINT: When reading the Gospels, take note of how often Jesus retreats to the wilderness to pray. Why does He do this? Why not pray inside of the cities and towns that He visits? What are some of the things that you can do to grow your relationship with Christ during your time in the wilderness this year?

THE PRESEASON

"The LORD will protect you from all evil; He will keep your soul. The LORD will guard your going out and your coming in from this time forth and forever."

Psalm 121:7-8

As August arrives, the heart of the Sportsman begins to stir. He knows that fall will not be far behind, and with it comes the opening of the hunting seasons. There is much work to be done before the fields and forests are ready for opening day. Food plots will have been planted and tended throughout the summer, but there are still many other things left to do.

The grass along the sides of logging roads will need to be bush-hogged, and the summer rains may have eroded the roads themselves, cutting deep channels into the soft red clay. Growing trees may have pushed some of the permanent ladder stands out of position, causing them to tilt in uncomfortable directions. Some of the trails will have been blocked by fallen trees, and there is always brush that needs to be trimmed.

With so much physical labor to be accomplished, it's easy to forget that we should do some work in the spiritual world as well. The Lord has given us this incredible wilderness to enjoy, and it's important that we remember to thank Him for it and to offer prayers for a safe and successful year in the deer woods. Mixing prayer and deer hunting – or even pre-deer hunting activities – is a wonderful thing, and this year I intend to do more of that than ever before.

I can remember one season a few years back when I went down to my lease in late August. I drove to every stand on the property and prayed over them all, asking that the men who hunted from each one would remain safe, that they would enjoy their time in the woods, and that they would see the hand of God as they spent time in His creation.

Stopping at every single stand that I could find, I asked that the men's thoughts would turn to God as they sat silently in the woods waiting for deer. I asked that each stand be productive and that the men who hunted from them would use wisdom as they saw deer and decided whether or not to make the shot. Though I am telling you about this now, I did the whole thing in secret, praying "in my closet" as Scripture instructs us to do. I did this not only because it seemed like a good idea, but because I saw it as a way of getting closer to God.

We have thirty or forty permanent stands on our lease, so you can imagine that praying over each one was an all day job. And so it was, but it also gave me the opportunity to get rid of any wasp nests that had been built into the corners of our box blinds, and to mark each stand on my GPS. This year I'm going to pray over my stands again, and as I do that I will take time to notice the direction that each stand is facing and will make a chart that will help me choose which stand to hunt according to which way the wind is blowing on a given day. I see no issue with being productive both spiritually and physically at the same time.

Some of our deer stands are starting to get old, and many of the wooden ladders are weakening. As I visit each stand during the preseason, I'll inspect the ladders for loose nails, hammering them back into place or adding new nails if necessary. Prayers for safety are particularly important at the older stands, and I will be diligent in asking God that no one get hurt in one of them. We haven't had an accident on the lease yet, and I don't want this year to be any different in that respect.

As I finish my day of prayer on the lease, I will stop at the main gate and ask for God's blessing upon the land as a whole. I'll ask that we continue to have access to this beautiful piece of property, and that we would use it in such a way as to glorify Him. I'll ask that He guard our coming and going on the property this year, and that He protect us from harm. There are dangers like rattlesnakes, coyotes and bears on this property, not to mention the occasional trespasser. I'll ask that God protect us in our encounters with any of them.

I'll close by asking that He bless even the animals themselves, growing majestic racks on the bucks and good size and health on the does. I'll ask that the turkeys have a successful breeding season, and that the birds and squirrels are plentiful. I'll even pray for the eagles that have nested in the pines across the road from the lake.

All of this is a way of connecting with both the Lord and the environment. Remembering God in our hunting endeavors draws us closer to Him. Paul instructs us to pray without ceasing, and praying over your stands and your deer woods are a good way to implement this. Walk with God not only in your daily life, but in all of your activities. You'll be glad that you did.

ACTION POINT: Pray over the stands on your deer lease this year. Pray specifically for safety during your hunts and for a bountiful year. Pray for men to come to Christ as they see His hand at work in the incredible world of the outdoors that surrounds them.

TARGET PRACTICE

"He trains my hands for battle, so that my arms can bend a bow of bronze."

Psalm 18:34

No matter how competent you are with your bow or rifle, it's important to take some time to refamiliarize yourself with your weapons each year before the season begins. When you are in the field, situations will arise where you'll need to be able to make a quick shot on an animal without having a lot of time to prepare yourself for it. Practicing with your weapons will get you ready for these situations.

A deer will appear in a small clearing or will cross the trail in front of your stand, and you'll need to be able to not only judge the animal quickly, but you'll also need to be ready to get your weapon in position as fast and as quietly as possible, and then follow up with an accurate shot. An intimacy with your weapons is essential for accomplishing this, and the only way to achieve that intimacy is to shoot them whenever you get a chance.

Each summer starting in late July, I'll get out my bow and go out to the target range that I've built in my back yard. My range is nothing more than a few stepping stones spaced at ten yard intervals, and my target is a foam deer that I was given as a birthday gift several years back. Summers are brutal in my part of the country, so my shooting sessions are limited to no more than a couple of dozen arrows a day.

By the time deer season comes around, I am comfortable enough with my bow to know its intricacies. I know how to nock an arrow without banging the riser, and the string silencers have been tuned to make the bow as quiet as possible. Muscle memory allows me to draw the bow efficiently and consistently, using the same anchor point with each shot. When a deer steps in front of my stand, I will be ready.

Similarly, we must also practice with our rifles and shotguns. Although I have a pretty good scope on my rifle, I do not let a year go by without going down to the range to make sure that it is still sighted in where I want it to be. Reticles can move over time, and I would never start a season without at least checking my zero before the first hunt.

I practice shooting from all manner of positions, both with the bow and the rifle. In my back yard, I'll lean around from behind trees to make a shot, or will hook one of my climbing stands to a pine tree and shoot a few shots from the same height that I'll be hunting at. At the rifle range, I'll shoot using a rest, but will also practice a few offhand shots just so that I'll be comfortable doing that if the need for a snap shot arises.

If you have a newer weapon, spend some extra time getting used to it. I bought a crossbow last year for the first time, and I am making an extra effort to shoot it whenever I get a chance. It handles differently than a bow or a rifle, so I often step out to my back deck and fire a couple of shots at a target that I've placed down in front of my garden. I want to be sure that I'm ready to use it when I first look through the scope at a deer.

Likewise, we must have an intimacy with God in order to fulfill our masculine roles in this world. We cannot lead our families well if we are not allowing God to lead us. We are unable to father our children unless we first permit God to Father us. Intimacy with God is developed through prayer and reading of Scripture, and by walking with Him in all that we do.

Intimacy is also developed by having conversations with the Lord. I often talk to Him as if He were sitting right beside me in the truck as I drive down to my lease. After all, in a manner of speaking, He is doing exactly that. I ask Him where I should go first when I get down to my property. I ask Him to lead me as I move a stand from one location to another. By talking to him in this fashion, my prayer life has improved in visible ways.

I am, for the first time, allowing God to be not only the Lord of my life, but also the Father who guides me in all of my endeavors. I ask Him to reveal those places in me that yearn for growth, and that have not reached maturity. He is responding in amazing ways.

Ask God to guide you in those areas of your life in which you lack spiritual maturity, as these areas can limit how closely you walk with Him. Ask Him specifically for wisdom, since James tells us that we lack wisdom simply because we don't ask for it. As you pray each day, you will grow closer to God and form that intimacy with Him that will allow Him to be your straight arrow as you walk towards True North.

ACTION POINT: Practice with your weapons as often as you can before the season opens. Become intimately familiar with them, and seek to know Christ in a similar manner.

CHOOSE YOUR EQUIPMENT WISELY

"For no man can lay a foundation other than the one which is laid, which is Jesus Christ. Now if any man builds on the foundation with gold, silver, precious stones, wood, hay, straw, each man's work will become evident; for the day will show it because it is to be revealed with fire, and the fire itself will test the quality of each man's work."

1 Corinthians 3:11-13

An old friend of mine once said something that struck me as very profound. What he said should have been obvious, but it was something that had never occurred to me before. It did, however, change my entire approach to the choices that I make when I am buying not only ammunition for hunting, but also other critical pieces of equipment.

"It strikes me as odd," my friend said, "when people spend so much money on rifles and scopes and then go out and buy the cheapest bullets that they can find."

This simple statement stopped me in my tracks, because it hit very close to home. For years I had skimped on my ammunition purchases, buying whatever brand of bullets that Wal-Mart had on sale at the time. The quality of such cartridges is extremely questionable, and immediately I realized that I had settled for mediocrity in the one place that I should have been willing to spend a little more money.

I had also been putting low quality optics on all of my rifles. I would spend four or five hundred dollars on a weapon and then put a $99 scope on it. It had never occurred to me before, but what I was doing was setting myself up for failure. I was handicapping myself through my equipment before I even got into the woods, and it was entirely my fault for making the choices that I was making whenever I purchased items for hunting.

At the time that my friend made that statement, I had just struggled through a difficult deer season, missing several shots at both deer and coyotes throughout the year, and I was even starting to question my skill with a rifle. The problem was that my very foundation was weak. I had spent lots of money on my deer lease, my camouflage clothing, my boots, and various other things, but my focus had been in the wrong place.

I had a decent rifle, but the scope that was attached to it was pretty much useless during the early morning and late afternoon hours. In the very hours that most deer move, my scope wouldn't pull in enough light to allow me to make a decent shot. Combine that with the fact that the bullets that I was using were very inconsistent, and the end result was an incredibly dismal season.

Over the next couple of years, I changed my strategy. Instead of buying the latest deer scent or camouflage pattern, I saved up my money and, once I could afford it, I put a much more expensive scope on my rifle. Having a better scope extended my hunting hours, allowing me to see deer earlier in the morning and later into the evenings. I know that quality optics can be extremely costly, but it almost always pays off in the end.

I also switched to a premium cartridge, which further increased my accuracy and consistency. The up-front costs were a little bit higher for me that year, but the results were well worth the money. My groups at the rifle range got much better, and my confidence in myself and my rifle grew by leaps and bounds.

In the long run I ended up with equipment that would last me a lifetime. My deer rifle has a great scope on it now; one that has worked well for me both in South Carolina and as far away as Africa. I'm still shooting the same bullets that I switched to after that dismal deer season, and my accuracy has remained extremely consistent. With those two changes, I was able to break out of my year-long slump and start making good shots on deer again.

In the same way, we must start with Christ as our foundation in all aspects of our lives. You can be the most religious person in the church, but if your religion is not built upon Christ then it is worthless. Peter tells us to make our calling and election sure, and indeed we must look inward to ensure that our faith is in Christ alone. When we start with a solid foundation, we can build upon it with great confidence and assurance.

ACTION POINT: If you don't know Christ, then you do not have a firm foundation. Just as the equipment that I was using during my worst year afield was handicapping me, your own foundation is likewise built upon shaky ground. Ask Him into your life today. You'll never be the same.

WORK DAYS

"For even when we were with you, we used to give you this order: if anyone is not willing to work, then he is not to eat, either. For we hear that some among you are leading an undisciplined life, doing no work at all, but acting like busybodies."

2 Thessalonians 3:10-11

Each season, a few weeks before opening day a bunch of us from my deer club get together for a work day on the lease. Every member is expected to attend and do their fair share of work. In my current club we are pretty lucky. Most of the guys show up and stay for the entire day, clearing brush, cutting shooting lanes, removing wasp nests from stands, and picking up rocks and other debris from our logging roads.

Other clubs that I have been in over the years have not had the caliber of men that are in my current club. On these other leases, there were always guys who would just stand around and talk while a handful of us worked our butts off to get the place in shape for the season. As you can imagine, this breeds resentment and anger among those upon whose shoulders the brunt of the labor falls on.

This is one way that problems start in hunting clubs and even in churches. In hunting clubs, the guys who work will ultimately get upset at those who are looking for a free ride, and trouble is not far behind. Factions are a dangerous thing, but they quickly form when things like this take place. Churches are the same way; a few people volunteer for all of the needs of the church while others never do anything to get involved. Before long a small group of people are doing so much work that they get burnt out, and the entire congregation suffers.

What is it that makes some men lazy and some hard workers? Why is it that one man digs a hole while six others stand around and watch? The Bible has a lot to say about work. In fact, if you read Genesis carefully you'll see that Adam was put in the garden to work it *before* the fall. While the NASB uses the term "cultivate," the NIV actually does say "work" in this verse. Work is not something that we do as a result of sin; it is something that we were called to at the very creation of the world itself.

In the verse from Thessalonians at the start of this chapter, Paul takes a very hard stance against those who don't work. If you don't work, he says, you don't eat. Although I don't like to see clubs get to the point where they have to penalize members, sometimes you have to put down rules like this that say that if you don't participate in a work day, you don't get to hunt on opening day.

For myself, I love a hard day of physical labor. My "real job" is one that does not involve any physical activity that is more difficult than typing on a keyboard, so at the end of a long week of work my body craves being outside working on this project or that one. My wife and I often joke that my days off (outside of hunting season) are harder than my actual work days. I love to get out on the lease and trim branches off of trails or remove fallen trees from our roads. It's just part of who I am.

ACTION POINT: Hard work is a blessing. Scripture tells us to do everything as unto the Lord, and He expects us to put our hearts into whatever we do. Keep this in mind whether you are working at your day job, mowing your lawn, or clearing brush at your deer lease.

OPENING DAY

"Now then, please take your gear, your quiver and your bow, and go out to the field and hunt game for me."

Genesis 27:3

In my part of the country, the archery deer season is the first one to open each year. In this particular section of South Carolina the season always comes in on the first of September, and I've been lucky enough to have only missed a single opening day in the last twenty years.

An opening day is a day of thanksgiving for me. It's a good time to ask the Lord for a safe and bountiful year in the field. At my house we live on venison year-round, so if I don't bring home four or five deer in a given season we'll find ourselves running out of meat sometime around the middle of the summer. So it's also a good time to be thankful to God for what He provided for us in previous years.

There are so many other things about this time of year that we can be thankful for. Men, thank your wife for supporting your hunting, and thank God for giving you such a wife. You can be all the more thankful if she joins you in the woods, but even if she doesn't, it's a rare and wonderful woman who understands our need to see another sunrise in the forest. My wife was raised among hunters, and she knows that it is a part of who I am. And she happily eats venison, so I am doubly blessed.

Wives, pray for your husbands. Ask that they would be wise in the woods, taking only safe shots and shooting only game that you intend to eat or to give to another. Pray that as your husband hunts for deer that he hunts even more for the heart of God, and that he would be the man that he has been called to be. Pray also that he enjoys himself and comes home refreshed, and a better man for having spent the day afield.

I always enter the woods on Opening Day with a sense of excitement and even a little bit of nervousness. I'm particularly careful when I climb up into a ladder stand on those first few hunts of the year. It's likely been quite some time since I've been up in one of these elevated stands, and it takes me a few times of going up and down before I regain my usual level of comfort with it.

I'm also more likely to step on sticks and make too much noise on those first few hunts. I think my eagerness to get into the woods gets the better of me, and I have to force myself to settle down and go slowly. Each year I promise myself that I'll take my time as I walk to my stand for that first hunt, and each year I end up breaking that promise. Maybe this year will be different.

Regardless, as I go afield this year on Opening Day I will remember to be thankful for the many things that I mentioned. I'll be sure to ask Christ to accompany me; to be my guide not only in the woods, but in all of my ways. I'll thank Him for allowing me to be a part of the club that I am in, and to have access to such a wonderful piece of property. I'll ask that the other hunters in my club, particularly those who are not Christians, would see the joy in my soul and ask me what it stems from. If they do, I'll be ready with my answer.

ACTION POINT: If you haven't made a pattern of it, thank your wife this year for the support that she gives you in your hunting and outdoor activities. Also take time to thank the Lord for the blessings that He has given you in these things. Thank Him for the land you hunt on, for the animals you hunt, and for the friends that you hunt with.

PRAYING BEFORE HUNTING

"Rejoice always; pray without ceasing; in everything give thanks; for this is God's will for you in Christ Jesus."

1 Thessalonians 5:16-18

I used to be diligent about praying each morning before I went into the deer woods. I still do pray once I'm in the stand, but in the last few years those prayers have felt more like an afterthought than a heartfelt conversation with the Lord. These days, it seems like I'll get settled into the stand, get my rifle in position, and then offer up a halfhearted *Thanks for letting me be in the woods again, Lord. Please keep my wife safe while I'm away, and may I have a bountiful day in the woods.*

I don't want to be that way. That's not a true prayer; it's one spoken out of a sense of duty rather than a true desire to talk to God. The way that I *want* to pray is in a much more authentic way. I want to boldly approach the Throne of God to which I have been given access through Christ. I want to stand by my truck with my brothers and lead them in prayer each morning before we part ways and head for our stands.

When I will be hunting alone on a given day, I will sometimes feel moved enough to pray that kind of prayer in the Jeep as I drive down the highway headed toward my lease. I'll pray aloud because I can focus better that way. I'll pray in specific ways, asking for specific things. I'll pray boldly and openly, knowing that there is no one else around to hear me. But more often than not, I just turn on my radio and listen to some audio book or podcast as I head down the road.

At home, my wife and I are careful to ask blessings over each meal that we eat together. We will also do this at restaurants, whether alone or with company. If we are eating with friends who do not seem moved to say a blessing on the meal, I will ask them if they mind if I say one for us. So why is it that I don't normally do the same thing when my buddies and I sit down to lunch at a local grill after the morning hunt? Both of the guys that I typically hunt with would be happy to have me do it, so why don't I?

The answer is simple. Prayer before a meal is (or was) the custom of the country. It's quite common to see someone asking a blessing over a meal even at a restaurant, but how often do men bow together before other things; things like hunting or fishing? It's not as common as it should be, and I want to learn to be the kind of man who will step out and make it happen.

So what is it inside of me that needs to change to make this kind of open prayer a larger part of my hunting experiences? Scripture clearly tells us that we are to pray about all things. It also tells us that we should not be ashamed of the Gospel, but in this case I don't believe shame is the problem.

It's fear. It's the same fear that paralyzed Adam when he stood with Eve in the Garden and watched as she ate the apple. It's the same fear that has been a part of man ever since. It's the thought that we are not enough, that what we do doesn't matter; that something as small as a blessing over a meal is not enough to make a difference. Men are notorious for keeping silent when they should speak; whole books have been written about this.

We keep silent when we are not confident in who we are. We fight the battles that we know we can win, but we remain quiet in those where we are not sure of the outcome. I have shared my testimony in front of an entire church and have not been nervous. I have made presentations at meetings to armies of coworkers, and I have spoken about my books on various radio shows. In none of those cases was I afraid to speak, because I was able to do so with confidence and assurance.

We should have that same assurance when it comes time to pray in front of others. The condition of our heart toward God is what matters, not the eloquence of the words that we say. Our prayers don't need to be impressive or filled with spiritual-sounding words; they just need to come from the heart. The best prayers are the ones where we just get down to business and seek the heart of God, and those are the kind that I want to learn to pray.

So this year when my buddies and I are ready to enter the woods, I'll ask them if they mind if I say a short prayer before we head to our stands. I'll pray brief, heartfelt prayers asking for safety and success, but more importantly I'll ask God to bring each of us closer to Him during our time in the woods. If I know my buddies as well as I think I do, I'm sure they'll be happy to oblige.

ACTION POINT: Pray with your friends before you go into the woods at least once this year. Pray from the heart, with the glorification of God in mind. It's ok to ask for success afield, but don't make that the sole focus of your prayer. And if you are successful, be sure to give thanks to God for the animal that He has provided for you.

TEMPTATION

"Keep watching and praying that you may not enter into temptation; the spirit is willing, but the flesh is weak."

Matthew 26:41

Temptation is something that we are faced with quite often in the deer woods. It comes in many forms, and it is not always easy to resist. Situations that tempt us occur almost every time we go afield, sometimes in subtle circumstances, but often in very overt ways.

In my particular deer club, members are allowed to bring guests as often as they like. The single restriction that we have is that visitors are only allowed to shoot does. If a guest shoots a buck, then he will be asked to leave and will not be welcomed back to the lease. The member himself is not disciplined in any way; the ostracism that he would face from the other members is usually punishment enough.

A couple of years ago I took my buddy Pete along with me on one of my hunts. He decided that he wanted to hunt in a stand way back at the far end of the lease, while I went to a box blind overlooking a small field surrounded by a forest of pines. I didn't see any deer that evening, and I didn't hear any shots from Pete's direction.

At sunset, when the hunt had ended, I drove over to Pete's blind to pick him up, and I found him standing on the side of one of our logging roads, shaking with excitement.

"I had a decision to make tonight," he told me, grinning. "I had to decide how much I like you."

When I asked him what he meant, he said that he had watched a ten point buck – an absolute monster – feed for over an hour. The buck was well within range of his rifle, and was standing broadside most of the time. Pete could have taken the shot at any time and he would have easily killed the buck of a lifetime.

Now, I know Pete pretty well, and he is a man of character. Knowing the rules of the club, he wasn't going to put our friendship to the test by taking that shot. Pete has never had the chance to kill a trophy buck before, so he did face temptation that evening, but there was never really a question as to whether he would do the right thing or not.

Sometimes though, temptation is not so easy to overcome. In my part of South Carolina, during the archery deer season only bucks are legal game. This is a bit different than what I have been used to for most of the years that I have spent hunting. In the past, any deer was legal with a bow, no matter how early in the season you shot it.

Archery deer season always starts on the first day of September, and the temperatures are still usually in the mid-90s at that time of year. The humidity is high and the mosquitoes are horrible. It's difficult to sit in a stand all day with the sweat pouring off of you while you watch doe after doe come into a field and you can do nothing but watch. There are many guys that would go ahead and take the shot, knowing that the chances of getting caught were very low. But as Christians first and sportsmen second, we must resist even this kind of temptation.

How many other times are we tempted in the woods? For years, I have wanted to shoot a bobcat. I'd love to have a full body mount, but the only shot I ever took at one completely missed the animal. The other opportunities that I have had have fallen outside of the predator hunting season.

I remember this one time that me and my friend Ted were hunting down on our little deer lease in Lancaster, SC. I was sitting in a box blind way out in a cutover, which looked down into a small food plot. A bit of movement in front of me caught my eye, and to my surprise a large bobcat walked into view and then sat down on the ground not ten feet in front of my stand. He had no idea that I was there.

I called Ted on the radio and asked him if bobcats were in season. I was pretty sure that they were not, and Ted quickly confirmed that. I told him that I had one in front of me, and oh man did I want to shoot him. The chances that I would be caught were very low. A taxidermist friend had once told me that he had never had a game warden ask him if a predator that he was mounting had been killed in season. But if I took that shot, I would always know that it was an illegal kill. I would know it, Ted would know it, the taxidermist would know it, and God would know it.

In the end I resisted, of course, but I would be lying if I told you that I knew all along that I wasn't going to take the shot. I even slipped the safety off of my rifle at one point and looked at that big cat through the scope. Before long though, I lowered my rifle and returned it to the safe position. To this day I have not yet taken a bobcat.

James tells us that God does not tempt us into sin. God may test our faith in many ways, but He will not do so through the temptation to sin. Remember that it was Satan who tempted Christ in the desert, not God. The temptations that we face in the woods likewise do not come from the Lord, and thus we must resist them, as Christ resisted Satan. Doing so gives glory to God, and helps us act with righteousness in a world that is filled with all manner of temptations.

> **ACTION POINT:** The temptation to take a trophy animal out of season or just across the property line on someone else's land is a common one for many hunters. Resist the urge to pull the trigger and just be thankful for having the opportunity to see such an animal.

A GIFT THAT LASTS A LIFETIME

"But earnestly desire the greater gifts. And I show you a still more excellent way."
1 Corinthians 12:31

Shortly after I got out of college, I took a temporary job in the mailroom at the headquarters of a regional grocery store chain. I wasn't making much money at the time, and I could not afford to do much more than pay my rent and buy the groceries that I needed each week. After a couple of years in that job, I got a chance to make a career move when I was hired as a computer programmer for a national bank, and before long I found myself making a little bit more money than I had ever had a chance to earn before.

One of the first things that I did with the extra income was to buy a lifetime hunting and fishing license. I had always said that I would get one if I ever had the money to do so, and being a young bachelor in a good job I suddenly found that I could afford the occasional investment like that. I was living in North Carolina at the time, and the license application for that state offered a place to write a small, personalized message which would be displayed on the license itself.

I couldn't think of anything to write, so I left that space blank. I was buying the license as a gift to myself, so it didn't seem appropriate to put any kind of message on the card, although I occasionally tried to come up with something interesting to put there. It wasn't until almost twenty years later that I thought of a good use for the space. I'll get to that in a minute.

When I bought my lifetime license, I wasn't dating anyone, nor was I even thinking about getting married. However, even at that young age I knew that if I was ever fortunate enough to have a son I would buy a lifetime license for him while he was still a baby. Many states offer infant licenses at a deeply discounted rate, putting them well within reach of most new parents. The caveat is that you only have a year or so to buy the license before the prices start to rise.

Now, as I approach my mid-forties, I finally have a child on the way. My son will be born in the heart of the coming deer season, and one of the first things that I will buy for him is a lifetime hunting and fishing license for South Carolina, the state that my wife and I currently live in. There's a small amount of risk involved, as there is some chance that he may not ultimately be interested in the outdoor sports, but I believe that it's a risk that's worth taking.

The interesting thing is that as his birth approaches, I've actually gone back and forth on whether or not I should actually get the license for him. I remember that when I turned sixteen, buying a hunting license for the first time was almost as big a deal for me as getting my driver's license. I still have that first license and the little North Carolina Hunting Regulations pamphlet that accompanied it. I have occasionally wondered if he'll miss out on the joy of actually going to the store and buying his first license, but in the end I think that he'll appreciate the lifetime gift more and more each year as he grows older.

I want to make sure that my son has plenty of opportunities to hunt and fish. Buying the license for him will at least ensure that he'll be able to do so in South Carolina with one less thing to worry about. So in the end, we will buy it for him, and I'll give it to him as a present on his sixteenth birthday. I won't even tell him we have it for him until that time, just to keep it a surprise.

As nice a gift as that will be, my wife and I will give him a far greater gift. We will raise him in a Christian home, where the Word is spoken on a daily basis. We will teach him Scripture, we will teach him to pray, and we will teach him masculinity as God meant it to be. We will raise him as a sportsman and as a warrior for Christ. In the end he will make his own choices and go in whatever direction he is called, but we will do our best to ensure that he chooses according to the wisdom of God.

And I've finally thought of something to write in the small space that is provided on the license for a message. A Scripture reference. It makes perfect sense; now the only thing to do is to choose a verse that provides wisdom and yet still relates to the outdoors. There are a great many that apply, and I still have plenty of time to think about that. And I will look forward to the day that I hand him his lifetime license and send him out into the field on his own.

ACTION POINT: Does your state offer infant lifetime hunting licenses? If so, consider investing in your child's future in this way. Whether you decide to do that or not, be sure to invest in the future of his soul by teaching him about the Lord.

THE STOLEN STAND

"The thief comes only to steal and kill and destroy; I came that they may have life, and have [it] abundantly."

John 10:10

Back in 2000, a few buddies and I got together and leased four or five hundred acres of land near Lancaster, SC. There were only four of us who were hunting on the property, and we could be pretty sure that each hunter could get three or four deer a year off of the property. It was a good club, but it was located in a heavily hunted area, and we had a lot of problems with trespassers over the years.

The property itself was bisected by a long power line right-of-way. We had fields planted every couple of hundred yards in this wide slash of land, and you could always see deer from the climbing stands that were locked to various trees up and down the line. We also had a couple of ladder stands in place, so there was good coverage for all of the food plots. Each stand was identified by a number on a large map that we had drawn, and it was common practice to refer to each stand by its numerical designation.

One day in December of 2001, I decided to drive down to the lease for an afternoon deer hunt. My buddy Ted had taken the morning off from work and had gotten a nice doe before I arrived, and he had already dropped it off at the processor and was back at the lease by the time that I got there. Before heading into the woods for the afternoon hunt, Ted and I spent a few minutes discussing where we each wanted to go.

I had gotten a brief look at a nice buck from one of the climbing stands on the power line a few days before, so I decided to spend the afternoon hunting from there. The stand that I was thinking of offered a 150 yard shot down to a food plot, and it was well hidden in a clump of pine trees. There was also a nice shooting rest nailed to a branch in the tree, and it was a very comfortable stand to hunt from. You didn't have to climb very high, and yet you could see more than two hundred yards of open space before you.

Wishing Ted good luck, I started the long walk from the Jeep down to the stand that I had chosen. I had hunted from this stand several times before, so I was a bit confused when I arrived at the appropriate location and did not see it hanging from its tree. I retraced my steps and saw that I was indeed in the right spot, but the stand itself was gone.

We always carried walkie-talkies in those days, so I got mine out and called Ted.

"Hey Ted, come in," I said. "I've got a bit of a problem. Did you happen to move stand number four?"

"No," he replied. "I would have mentioned it when you told me where you were planning on hunting."

"Well," I returned, "it's gone."

Looking closely around the base of the pine tree, I found the lock that had held the stand in place. It had been pounded with a hammer, and it quickly became obvious that the stand had been stolen. I cursed and kicked at the tree. I thought about just sitting on the ground beside it and just finishing the hunt from there, but then I remembered that there was another climber 100 yards behind me that looked down into the same field. That seemed to be the best choice, so I walked back up the hill and took a look at the stand.

This other climber was a good bit more exposed than mine had been, the distance to the field was longer, and there was no good rest to shoot from. Nevertheless, I decided to make the best of the situation so I climbed up the tree, attached my safety belt, and got settled in for the hunt.

I was disgusted at the way that one hunter could steal from another without giving it a second thought, but I tried to put that out of my mind as I prepared myself for the afternoon hunt. I was pretty sure that I wouldn't see anything, because I had made quite a bit of noise when I called Ted to tell him that the stand had been stolen.

Almost immediately, however, one large doe and two smaller ones walked into the field that I was watching. The lead doe was quite large, and I decided to go ahead and make the shot. Slipping off the safety, I moved my rifle into position, breathed out, and then squeezed the trigger.

Click.

Still frustrated over the loss of my stand, I had forgotten to chamber a round once I was safely in the tree. I quickly worked the bolt and jacked a cartridge into the hole. The deer was presenting me with a good broadside shot, so I again breathed out and squeezed the trigger. The gun fired this time, but there was no visible reaction from the deer. I had missed her cleanly. I chambered another round and tried again.

This time I saw dirt splash up from the ground behind the deer which, to my surprise, still did not run away. I put a third round into the chamber and forced myself to slow down. I had one bullet left, so I had to make this one count. Taking three deep breaths in slow succession, I checked my aim and fired again. This time the deer collapsed in a heap, dead where she stood.

Shaking, I climbed down from the tree and went down to inspect the deer. Though I had made a killing shot, the entrance wound was not where it should have been. It was clear that my scope needed adjusting, and after a quick check I found that one of the screws on the base of the mount was loose.

Although the day turned out ok, it was marred by the theft of one of my favorite climbing stands. I wondered again how one hunter could do something like this to another, but there is dishonesty everywhere in this world. This thief had done more than take my stand though; he took my trust as well. I never again felt comfortable leaving a stand locked to a tree in the woods.

How much more does our true enemy Satan steal from us? Scripture makes it clear that he has the ability to attack even those who believe in Christ. I didn't use a strong enough lock on my stand, but in fighting spiritual battles we have the strongest lock of all: the blood of Jesus Christ. It has the power to bind the enemy away from us, but we must pray it against him on a daily basis. While I may not trust a simple Masterlock on my stands in the future, I *will* trust in *the* Master when it comes to matters of spiritual warfare.

> **ACTION POINT:** Always remember that there is an enemy who is set against you and against everything that you stand for. Do battle with him using the armor of God and the blood of Jesus Christ.

WE ARE OUR OWN WORST ENEMY

"Now I exhort you, brethren, by the name of our Lord Jesus Christ, that you all agree and that there be no divisions among you, but that you be made complete in the same mind and in the same judgment."

1 Corinthians 1:10

Several years ago, my friend Arnold was telling me about an argument that was taking place on some internet forums that were hosted by the South Carolina Department of Natural Resources. It seems that a bunch of guys who hunted deer with dogs were clashing with guys who only hunted from stands and did not use dogs.

The still-hunters, as they are known, were upset because the dogs from the adjacent clubs were leaving their own property and were chasing deer over onto the lands that were being still-hunted. Dogs obviously can't read "no trespassing" signs, but the belief was that the dog owners should be in better control of their animals during their hunts.

I got involved in the dispute as something of an impartial observer, and in the end a group of us met at a local BBQ joint to discuss the problem at length. It was an informal meeting, with representation from still hunters, dog hunters, and even three game wardens. We tossed ideas for solutions to this problem back and forth for several hours, but in the end nothing was really accomplished.

Ultimately the two groups remained at odds with each other. The dog hunters felt like the still hunters were trying to shut down a long-standing South Carolina tradition, and the still hunters felt that the dog hunters did not have any respect for property lines. The arguments continue to rage, and I doubt that dog hunting will survive for too many more years in this state. They are outnumbered, and in the end they will lose this battle.

This is not the first time that I have seen hunters clash with each other. Go to any internet site or gathering of sportsmen and you'll witness heated exchanges on any number of topics. Baiting deer with corn is a really good example of this. There aren't many topics that polarize hunters more than this one, and I have seen the vilest epithets being applied to people on both sides of this argument as they trade insults.

Guys who have no problem pouring doe urine on the ground or hunting over a field full of wheat will sneer at guys who hunt over bait. Making mock scrapes is fine with them, but put some corn out and suddenly all of the challenge is gone and it's no longer a hunt, at least in their minds. The hunters who use corn fire back that the only reason the non-baiters don't use it is because it's illegal in their counties. The whole situation is just crazy.

I've even seen bowhunters turn up their noses at people who prefer to use a rifle or even a crossbow to hunt deer. Just as fly fishermen sometimes look down at spincasters, bowhunters can be a fairly snobby lot. If I anger you by saying that, then you may just be one of the people that I'm talking about. As amazing as it sounds, there are divisions among us simply because of our choice of weapon. If we ever lose the right to hunt, we can blame it on quarrels from within rather than pressure from the outside. This infighting simply has to stop.

In order to present a united front, we must learn to deal peacefully with each other in all things. We must police our ranks, and we've got to learn to resolve our differences with grace and – dare I say it – tolerance. At the risk of sounding liberal, we must learn to tolerate practices that we may not like, such as hunting with dogs or baiting deer where legal. That's not to say that we should put up with anything and everything, but when hunters are arguing over legal practices, sportsmen as a whole suffer.

Perhaps the dog hunters could run their hounds once per week and give them a rest for a few days, allowing the still hunters a chance to get out into the woods without having their hunts disrupted. Keeping tighter control over where the dogs are cast would also go a long way in preventing the trespassing that happens from time to time. And if you don't like the practice of hunting deer over corn, don't do it! But also refrain from criticizing those who do.

The same holds true among Christians. In many cases, we are our own worst enemies. The worst behavior that I have ever seen among adults has happened within the walls of a Baptist church. I've seen entire families that have been split down the middle as arguments erupted within a congregation, and more than one church has been brought to ruin by things like this.

And by all means there are certainly times where we must speak up. When the offense is spotlighting deer or preaching that crosses out of the boundaries of sound doctrine, then by all means we must fight for what is right. But when the issues are simply matters of personal preference we must either keep silent or air out our differences respectfully. This is the only way that we will survive.

ACTION POINT: Before criticizing a hunting practice that you don't personally agree with, ask yourself if you will cause division among our ranks by speaking out. If so, keep silent. Refamiliarize yourself with First Corinthians and think about what triggered Paul's letter to the church at Corinth.

CROSSING FENCES

"Do not move the ancient boundary or go into the fields of the fatherless"

Proverbs 23:10

When I was a kid growing up outside of Charlotte, our house was just down the road from the fields of the Rea farm, one of the largest farms that was still in existence in that area in the early eighties. On fall afternoons when school let out I would often grab the little 20 gauge shotgun that my parents had given me, stick a box of shells in my bird hunting vest, and walk down the road to the bob-wire fence that marked the edge of the Rea property.

Though I did not have permission to hunt their fields, I would spread the wires of the fence apart, then slip through the opening and go sit on the edge of the field and take shots at the occasional dove that flew over. I wasn't alone in my transgressions; other neighborhood boys would often join me as we stalked these forbidden fields and forests.

We never got caught in the fields, and I'm sure the owners didn't even have any idea that we were out there. Their house was quite far away from where we were, and they never knew that they had been wronged. But sin against them we did, although we were just boys and didn't mean any harm. We didn't damage the crops or leave trash in their fields, but we did enter them without asking permission.

All of this came rushing back to me once when I was on a kudu hunt in Africa. A group of us – myself, the professional hunter, and our tracker – were walking down a long logging road on the way to a favored blind from which we would hunt kudu that evening. The red dust of the African soil puffed up in swirls around our feet as we trudged down the road. A low bob-wire fence ran parallel to the road, and occasionally we would pass large holes where bushpigs and warthogs had dug their way under the fence.

Without warning, a large male warthog suddenly appeared in the road a hundred yards down in the direction that we were walking. Zwei, the professional hunter, held up his hand, indicating that we should be still. He looked intently at the animal for a moment or two, and then turned to speak to me.

"Shoot him as soon as he turns," he said.

"We've seen a lot of warthogs," I replied. "What's special about this one?"

"Shoot him!" Zwei exclaimed.

Obeying orders, I chambered a round and quickly squeezed off a shot. The pig squealed, and then began to run down the road as quickly as he could. When he turned to run under the fence, I fired another shot. The pig disappeared from sight as I recovered from the recoil of my rifle.

"Let's go," Zwei said, breaking into a run. I followed as quickly as I could, and we soon arrived at the place where the warthog had darted under the fence.

A large splash of blood was visible in the dust, and we could see more of it leading into the brush on the other side of the fence. From what we could tell, the warthog was hit hard and should not have been able to go very far into the woods.

Zwei spoke the words that I had been dreading. "We cannot go onto that property without permission, even to recover your pig."

In a flash, I remembered all of the fences that I had crossed – legally and illegally – in my hunting career. I wondered if I was being paid back for my earlier sins. I was, however, quite relieved when Zwei pulled out his cell phone and said that he would make a phone call to try to get permission for us to cross over to retrieve my animal.

In the end we did indeed cross the fence, and we found the animal lying dead on the ground just fifty yards into the brush on the neighboring property. It turned out to be the warthog of a lifetime, with thirteen inch tusks and razor sharp bottom teeth. As thankful as I was to recover the animal, I couldn't help but cringe as I thought about those earlier trespasses.

We could have crossed that fence and retrieved my warthog without making the cell phone call and the property owners would likely have never know of our transgression, just as the Rea family never knew about the dove hunting that we had done on their farm thirty years before. God, however, would have seen our action, and though we would have felt like we were justified, indeed we would not have been breaking the law.

One of the things that makes me the angriest as a hunter is catching a trespasser on my deer lease. And even as I write this, I can see the irony in that, as I have just discussed occasions where I myself have crossed fences and boundaries onto lands that I did not have access to. As I have grown older, though, I am no longer tempted by such forbidden fruits, or at least I am better able to resist their siren's call. Fences like these are safe from me now, and though things may look better on the other side, I will remain content to hunt only on the lands that I have access to.

ACTION POINT: Remember that God is watching your every action. He will act as the judge for those whose lands that you trespass on, even if they are not aware of your transgression. Respect private property, and if you must retrieve an animal that has run onto someone else's land, get permission to do so before you cross the property line.

CAMOUFLAGE

"He said, 'I heard the sound of You in the garden, and I was afraid because I was naked; so I hid myself.'"

Genesis 3:10

When I first started hunting, there were really only two camouflage patterns available: woodland green or woodland brown. Most guys wore the green variety, but some of the old-timers that I ran into favored brown. Either way, there wasn't much choice when it came to picking out your hunting clothes for the new season.

Things have changed in the modern world, and there are now more patterns available than I could begin to list. And although I have my favorites and I wear them regularly, I often wonder just how necessary this stuff really is. It's obviously important to break up your outline in the woods, but this can be done by sitting behind a brush pile or choosing a tree that has plenty of cover behind it when setting up your stands.

My buddies and I often talk about how camouflage is really for the hunters themselves. It gives us a commonality; a way to recognize each other when we cross paths in the little stores and grills that mark the countryside where we do our hunting. It is the uniform of our sport, and I proudly wear my own camouflage whenever I am afield.

But thinking about camouflage also makes me think about how we as men hide our true selves. Adam hid from God because he had become aware of his nakedness, and men as a whole have felt naked ever since. We fear being exposed as phonies; as something less than real men, so we put on these personas that are images of masculinity, but are not who we authentically are. We wear our camouflage not just in the woods, but in our homes, our offices, and particularly in our church lives.

Many years ago, when my wife first mentioned the idea that we should start going to church, I resisted her. The idea of being around *church people* revolted me. I wanted to be in the presence of people who lived authentic lives, who talked about real things that were going on in their lives and who would say more than "God is just blessing my socks off." I didn't want to go into a building where I would have to smile and make small talk with people who would do nothing more than talk about the weather or how good God was.

In the end I gave in and agreed to go with her to church. It was a life changing decision, and though she led us in that effort I took the reins from her – sometimes gently, sometimes not – and assumed my place as the spiritual leader of our home.

We were fortunate in that we found a church home where we could share our lives with the people around us, and where the small talk is kept to a minimum. I've found a group of men among whom I can be who I really am, and not hide behind the camouflage of churchiness. I do not need to wear my fig leaf when I am with them, and though getting to this point has been a journey, it has been one that was worth taking.

There are a handful of books that have helped me along my way, and I highly recommend John Eldredge's *Wild at Heart*, as well as *The Barbarian Way* by Erwin McManus. These books helped me understand what freedom in Christ is all about, and they have helped me to remove my camouflage and move toward a more authentic life.

ACTION POINT: What kind of camouflage do you wear as a man? As a Christian? Ask God to help you take off that camouflage and lead you into an authentic life where you truly experience freedom in Him.

MOVING BEYOND THE CROSS

"For though by this time you ought to be teachers, you have need again for someone to teach you the elementary principles of the oracles of God, and you have come to need milk and not solid food."

Hebrews 5:12

As a young teenager I used to hunt squirrels and doves on a small piece of land that was owned by my friend Robert's father. To get to the property we had to walk about a half mile on the paved road leading out of our neighborhood, and then we'd go for another full mile on a little dirt road that led to the fenced in tract of land that his family owned.

Small game was plentiful on the property, and I can clearly remember killing my first squirrel in the hardwoods on the northern end of the land. The dove hunting was good too, and once in a while we would even jump a covey of quail that lived in the tall grass near the creek that bordered the property.

The creek that ran along the edge of the property was wide and deep, and on the other side of it was a huge tract of woods that was inhabited by larger game like raccoons, bobcats, and even deer. We weren't supposed to set foot onto that land, but one fall afternoon when he got tired of chasing the squirrels Robert suggested that we cross the creek and see if we could jump a deer.

I thought about the idea for a few minutes, but in the end I told him that I didn't think it was a great idea. If we ended up killing a deer, Robert's father certainly would have known that we had broken the rules by going onto property that we weren't supposed to be on, since his own land was surrounded by a high fence that even deer couldn't jump over. Robert agreed with me after giving it a little bit more thought, and we ended up staying on our side of the water.

Although we had done the right thing by not crossing over the creek to hunt on those forbidden lands, I couldn't help but stare wistfully at the tall oaks on the far side of the water. The trees were full of acorns, and the habitat was perfect for deer. Robert eventually did get permission to hunt in those woods, and he got his first deer there not long after suggesting that we slip across the creek to hunt. He invited me along with him on a couple of hunts on that now available property, but I still refused. I think I must have been a little bit timid at the time, and didn't want to move past the world that I was familiar with.

I was thinking about those old times the other day, and I saw a parallel between stopping at the creek and stopping at the cross of Christ. I had accepted Christ into my life at a fairly young age, but after that I did what a lot of Christians do. I got saved, and then went on with my life. I failed to move beyond the cross, just as I had refused to cross the creek when a legitimate opportunity arose.

Many of the men I know would be quick to tell you that they are saved and that they have a relationship with Christ, but most of them have gone no further than that. They make no effort to read their Bibles or to learn more about what being a Christian really means. There is a much larger life waiting for us beyond the cross, a life of adventure and learning, but to get there we have to see that Christ did more for us than just ransom our souls. He says that He came to set the captives free, and indeed He did. He opened the door for us, but we have to take the first steps to move into that freedom ourselves.

Many Christian men do not understand that Christianity is about more than knowing where we will go when we die. It's much greater than a choice between heaven or hell; it's an invitation to live a life of freedom such as we have never known before. In Galatians, Paul tells us that it was for such freedom that Christ redeemed us and that we should no longer be burdened by a yoke of slavery.

What slavery is it that he is referring to other than the slavery of sin? We must learn not to cling to our lives of sin; to turn from the things that are not of God, but we should also not get too burdened by it when we do sin. We're all going to miss the mark from time to time, and when we do we must remember that we have been set free from the penalty of that sin. Yes, we must repent of it and yes, we must not remain in those things in our lives that put distance between us and God, but we also must not let them bog us down and rob us of our freedom.

When the permission finally came for me to hunt in those beautiful oaks beyond the creek, I did not step into that freedom; I chose to stay in the comfortable place that I was familiar with. In that freedom, Robert got his first deer, and I hunted in vain on overcrowded game lands for the next ten years without getting one myself.

I lived the first years of my Christian life without understanding what freedom meant. I had to step beyond my salvation and go deeper into a relationship with Christ before I began to comprehend what the true offer of Christianity was about, and it is only now that I am beginning to live in the freedom that He has given me. Scripture often compares drinking milk with the spiritual life of an immature believer, and by my own admission I drank that milk far too long.

ACTION POINT: How far have you gone in your relationship with Christ? Have you stopped at the cross, or are you going deeper; not just reading your Bible but studying it, praying boldly before the throne of God, and living a life of freedom? Think about this, and if you are still "drinking milk," what will it take to move to "solid food?"

TIPPING EXTRA

"Give, and it will be given to you. They will pour into your lap a good measure — pressed down, shaken together, [and] running over. For by your standard of measure it will be measured to you in return."

Luke 6:38

Although we sportsmen know that hunting is a noble and honorable pursuit, there are many people who don't understand the very core rule of conservation, which is that some animals must die in order that others may live. If you've watched any hunting shows on TV or have read any outdoor magazines over the last twenty years, you know that there are large numbers of people who are devoted to ending all forms of hunting. Although these anti-hunters do not represent the majority, they have a loud voice that we must learn to combat in the appropriate manner.

As a rule, Americans in general actually support the idea of hunting. It's the hunters themselves that they don't like. For years we've let sitcoms and the left-wing media portray us as drunken slobs who leave a mess in the woods and who don't care about where our bullets go after they leave the barrel of our guns. They don't understand that it is we who are the true environmentalists; for without an environment, we have nowhere to hunt. I've never yet seen a sportsman who didn't love the fields and woods of our great country, and who didn't recognize the beauty of the unspoiled wilderness.

I've often wondered what we can do to improve the image of hunters as a whole. I believe that it must start at the local level on a seemingly small scale; we must win the hearts of the individuals that we encounter in our daily lives. There are several things that we can do to accomplish this, and if each of us presents a positive picture of what it means to be a hunter every time we go afield, public perception will begin to improve.

Let's look at my deer lease as an example of what I am talking about. I am a member of a group of a dozen or so men who lease 1800 acres in the northeastern part of Kershaw County, South Carolina. Our lease is bordered by an upscale lakefront neighborhood, and this gives us a prime opportunity to show that we as hunters are good stewards of what we have been entrusted with.

At the main entrance to our club, we have a large map that shows the location of all of our stands. Each hunter is expected to tag in before he goes into the woods, and then remove his tag at night when he leaves the stand. By the very nature of it, this little map board has become a gathering place for the club members, and many of us occasionally eat our lunches at the board, or just stop and chat between the morning and the afternoon hunts.

When we first took ownership of the club, the map board area was an absolute mess. The previous group of hunters often left trash lying around on the ground, and the entire place had a dilapidated look and feel. It wasn't befitting of such a beautiful piece of property. When our group took over the lease, the first thing we did was to clean up that area and put a large garbage can in place so that we'd have somewhere to put our trash.

At one time I suggested to my club members that we take it a step farther – that sometime during the spring or summer we all get together and, wearing our camouflage and orange vests, actually do a roadside cleanup of the entire stretch of neighborhood that our lease borders. The neighbors would likely be delighted to see us doing this, and it couldn't do anything but foster goodwill between us and them. We have yet to actually put this plan into action, but I'm still hoping that I can convince some of the guys to participate.

The point is that I want our club to be an asset to the neighborhood. I want those who live there to be glad that they have a conscientious group of hunters in their midst, and by doing so increase the positive perception that they have of sportsmen as a whole.

Another thing that I like to do to improve our image is one that is much easier than an organized roadside cleanup. When I go hunting I typically go for the entire day, so I have to do something about lunch. We usually eat at a little restaurant that is just down the road from our lease, but sometimes we'll drive into Camden or Lancaster for a better meal. Regardless, we always wear our camouflage clothing into the restaurant, and I make sure that we always leave an extremely nice tip for the waitress.

Now, there are a couple of caveats to this. The old way of thinking was that we should not wear our camouflage in public. However, this is what marks us as sportsmen, so I think that it's a good idea to keep it on when going to the local eateries. The key is that there should be no deer blood showing on your clothing, nor should you look like a slob in your outfit. If there's blood, change into a backup set of clothes before going into a restaurant. Tuck in your shirt and be sure to look and act like a gentleman.

A generous tip is the most important part of this idea. If you normally tip a dollar for a hamburger and fries, leave two or even three. It's not money that you'll likely miss, but it adds up for the waitress, and don't think that she won't recognize the fact that it's hunters who tip her the best. Give them a reason to be glad to see you.

Now I know that the first argument that a lot of guys have against this whole idea is that they don't want their camouflage clothing to end up smelling like a restaurant. I'm not concerned about this myself, as I have always been pretty blessed in my deer hunting and usually have incredibly bountiful seasons. However, if this does bother you, then why not throw an extra set of camouflage into your truck before you head for the woods, and then wear them when you go into town for lunch.

Let's stop here and apply this idea to our lives as Christians. In a recent sermon, my pastor asked the question "Do you know what the restaurants in Gastonia think about Christians? They hate to see us coming. They hate it because we are rude and stingy. They would rather see the rest of the pagan world come into their buildings than a bunch of church people."

He made a good point. The more traditional of us still dress up for church on Sunday mornings, and our church clothing identifies us as Christians just as quickly as our camouflage shows us to be hunters. The fact that many of us bow our heads and ask a blessing over our meals is another identifying mark on us as the body of believers.

It's hard for me to understand how we can go to church and hear the Word of God preached, and then act like idiots once we leave the sanctuary and head out into the world. The only thing that this does is give our enemies ammunition to use against us. We should fight this battle in the same way that we do as hunters.

When you eat your Sunday dinner at one of the local restaurants in your city, again, tip extra and act like a gentleman. Think twice before making a rude remark to the waitress, and be forgiving if the kitchen messes up your order. Make these people glad that you chose their restaurant to eat in. The only thing that these ideas can do is improve the public perception of us as Christians and as sportsmen.

ACTION POINT: God has a lot to say about generosity. If it's so important to Him, then it should be important to us as well. If you're wearing your uniform, be it camouflage clothing or your Sunday best, be sure to not only look the part, but act it as well. Give a generous tip, and let the rest of the world know that you and your kind are an asset.

INVISIBLE

"For since the creation of the world His invisible attributes, His eternal power and divine nature, have been clearly seen, being understood through what has been made, so that they are without excuse."

Romans 1:20

A couple of years ago I was browsing through the hunting clothing at my local Wal-Mart when I came across a camouflage baseball cap that I really liked. The word "Invisible" was embroidered onto the face of the cap, but it was done using stitching that matches the color of the cap itself, so in effect the word itself is almost invisible. Running along the front of the bill was the verse above from Romans. I tried it on, and as the fit was perfect I couldn't resist buying it.

That cap became my primary hunting hat for the next several years. I loved the double meaning of the word "invisible" on the cap; it pointed me first toward God, but it also reflected the fact that the purpose of camouflage is to render us invisible in the woods. I kept hoping that one of my buddies would notice the Scripture on the bill and ask me about it, but no one ever did. Regardless, every time I wore the cap it gave me occasion to think about what that Scripture means.

The message of the verse is that God has revealed Himself through His very creation, and that men have no excuse for not recognizing the fact that the universe is a created thing. One has only to take a hard look at the world around him to see that it is not a thing that occurred by accident. The complexity of life, the beauty of nature, and the perfection of physics are clear evidence of the existence of God. Proponents of the theory of evolution may disagree, but they are only fooling themselves if they think that their proposition can fully explain the cosmos.

What this verse of Scripture does not imply is that seeing the evidence of God and believing in Him through what He has obviously created brings you to a saving knowledge of Him. We still need Christ; but we can at least see that God exists by seeing the complexity of His universe. James tells us that even the demons believe that there is one God, but that this does not give them salvation. But taking it beyond the complexity that is required to keep things running smoothly, look at the beauty of the world. A field of flowers or the peaks of distant mountains are empirically beautiful. One does not need to be told this to recognize it as the truth.

I love what Ted Nugent once said on his *Spirit of the Wild* television show. He was in the process of field dressing a deer on camera, and as he removed the entrails he held them up for the viewer to get a look at. "Do you see this?" he asked. "This is a liver. Explosions don't make livers. God made that." I laughed so hard at this that I rewound the video on my DVR several times just to allow the truth of what he said to hit home.

My cap has just about worn out now, and I've tried to find another one like it but so far have not had any luck. I've got my eye on a different one now though, which says "Be Still" in small letters on the face of the cap. That one points the wearer to the Psalms, which is probably for the best. I've contemplated the Romans verse quite often over the years, and it's probably about time that I move on to another piece of Scripture.

ACTION POINT: Look for the work of the invisible Hand of God in the simple beauty of the outdoors the next time that you are afield. Scripture tells us that God's work is clearly seen, even though He Himself is not.

THE IMPORTANCE OF SOUND DOCTRINE

"For if one comes and preaches another Jesus whom we have not preached, or you receive a different spirit which you have not received, or a different gospel which you have not accepted, you bear [this] beautifully."

2 Corinthians 11:4

A couple of years ago I was at a sportsman's banquet down near the town of Lancaster, South Carolina. The speaker was giving a seminar about hunting monster bucks, and I found myself questioning many of the things he said. By all appearances, this fellow had the right credentials, having had several articles published in the most popular hunting magazines.

Nevertheless, the advice that he was giving seemed less than sound to me. Some of the things that he said seemed to have the ring of truth to them, but upon careful consideration I found that I disagreed with almost every point he made. Now I certainly don't claim to be the best and most knowledgeable deer hunter out there, but I have killed my share of decent animals over the years, so I felt like I had my years of success in the woods as a solid base for disagreeing with the things that he said.

For example, he seemed to think that rubs on small trees were always made by young bucks, and that a rub line on saplings wasn't worth a second look. This simply isn't true. I've seen mature deer rubbing on cedar trees that were no more than an inch or two in diameter. In my experience, when a buck gets the urge to rub on a tree he's going to pick the closest one at hand.

This fellow also echoed a popular commercial of the time by saying that the biggest bucks only move at dawn and dusk, and thus hunting in the middle of the day is a complete waste of time. I think most of us know that this is not true, and that many trophy bucks are killed in the hours after lunch when most hunters have already left the woods. You can't pigeonhole deer behavior; they're going to do what they want to do.

Another example he mentioned was that you might as well stay home on windy days, because the deer are going to stay put. If they can't pinpoint the direction that a smell is coming from, they won't move. One of the best hunting days that I had last year was in the remnants of Hurricane Ida as it passed through our area. The rain came down sideways all morning, and the wind was some of the worst that I'd ever seen in the deer woods. However, I saw at least seven deer from the comfort of my box blind that day, and at least one of them was a good sized buck.

It's important, therefore, that you base your hunting on sound doctrine. Sure, you should pay attention to the wind direction when you chose your hunting location for the day, but that shouldn't be the ultimate element that influences your decision. You have to factor in what you know about the nature of deer themselves, and use past experience to help you decide how and where to hunt on a given day.

When it comes to our Christian lives, we are lucky that we have a solid basis on which to make our choices. We have the Bible as the final word on the nature and character of God, but we need to learn to rely on it when we consider the importance of sound doctrine in our lives.

I am greatly concerned that there has been a major falling away from sound doctrine in the modern church, and particularly among the men of the church. The Bible mentions a great apostasy in the last days, and I'm of the opinion that we are seeing the start of that. You only have to look at some of today's television preachers or supposedly Christian authors to see what I'm talking about.

The prosperity gospel is a great example of this. The preachers of this false doctrine would have you believe that you merely have to ask God for wealth and He will give it to you. They tell you that wealth and happiness are the things that God most wants for you, and that you only have to speak for them to become reality. So many people are deluded by this kind of teaching because it feels positive, but it has no basis in Scripture. Indeed, Scripture tells us that we should not store up treasures on this earth. God's ultimate desire is for us to be holy as He is holy, and to thereby glorify Him.

Another example that really saddens me is the way a certain fictional book has gained acceptance among Christians in the past few years. I was hanging out with a couple of guys for a while who seemed to see this book as providing a wonderful view of the Trinity. In the book, a man encounters each of the Trinity in physical form at a cabin in the woods, and they teach him about how they interact with each other. I was greatly distressed to see the way people accepted the book without questioning the validity of the doctrine that it presented.

The views in this book are, when examined carefully, bordering on absolute blasphemy. The holiness of God is completely forgotten as He is reduced to cooking meal after meal for the others in the story. Indeed, the book seems to espouse a Universalist view which is in complete contradiction with what we know about the nature of God from the Bible. Although I had hoped to have a chance to speak out on this subject and ask my friends if they had given the theology much thought, that opportunity never arose.

Unfortunately, we don't have a Bible for deer hunting the way we do for our Christian walk. However, we do need to have a solid base for the things we believe; not only about God but also about the way we go about chasing deer in the woods. We must think before we believe.

ACTION POINT: When presented with new information about the nature and character of God, compare it with what you know about Him from reading your Bible. Is what you are hearing really in sync with what Scripture says? Consider each new piece of information carefully and be slow to incorporate new ideas into your Christian worldview.

WE EAT GOOD AROUND HERE

"A voice came to him, 'Get up Peter, kill and eat!' But Peter said, 'By no means, Lord, for I have never eaten anything unholy and unclean. Again a voice [came] to him a second time, 'What God has cleansed, no [longer] consider unholy.'"

Acts 10: 13-15

Back in my college days, it was a rare thing for me and my roommates to have any venison to eat. Although I was doing a good bit of deer hunting at the time, I had yet to kill a deer, and the only meat we got was what was donated to us by friend of ours who was a much more successful sportsman than me. We always made a big deal over it whenever we cooked the chops that he provided for us; it seemed "cool" to be eating deer meat, and we were always very vocal about what we were having that night.

As I became more successful in my trips afield, venison started showing up in the freezer on a regular basis, and some of the "uniqueness" of eating it disappeared. Nowadays deer meat is standard fare at our house, and I hardly even think about the fact that we're eating something wild when I serve it to my family. I haven't bought ground beef in years, and although I still buy steaks and brisket at the grocery store, that's about the extent of the meat that we purchase.

Recently I was trying to put together a list of all of the wild game that I've eaten over the years. There's a restaurant down in Greenville, South Carolina that serves game, and a lot of the wild stuff that I've had in the last few years has come from there. At that restaurant I've dined on antelope, bison, caribou, elk, kangaroo and yak, among other things. And in case you're wondering, of all of the meats that I've eaten there in Greenville, I'd say the best would be either the kangaroo or caribou. While I love eating there, it just doesn't beat the wild game that comes fresh from the field.

When I was on safari in Africa I got to sample the meat from several different antelope species. Eland was easily the best, and one night we ate both T-bone steaks and smoked sausage from that big animal. Kudu also proved to be a wonderfully tasty piece of meat, and impala was similar in taste and texture to our own whitetail deer. The meat that I liked the least was gemsbok, which had an unusual flavor that was completely different from anything else that I've eaten. My one regret is that I didn't get to try any meat from the zebra that I killed. The safari was over before it was ready for the grill, but I heard later that it went over quite well with the next group of hunters that was in camp.

Back on the North American continent, caribou is my favorite game meat. Elk is a close second, and I prefer the taste of mule deer to whitetails. I've been lucky in that both of the wild boar that I've killed have been very tender and tasty, as I've heard that they can sometimes have an unpleasant odor and flavor. Of the game birds that I've eaten, grilled breast of wood duck was unbeatable, with quail following closely behind.

I'm not much of a fish eater, but I'll go for a piece of dolphin or wahoo if the opportunity presents itself. Tuna steaks are another favorite seafood of mine, and I'll always have a fondness for calabash shrimp and fried clam strips. Although I don't care much for freshwater fish, some of the best meals that I've ever eaten have been bass or crappie that went straight from the lake to the frying pan. Salt and pepper catfish are good too, and though I don't eat them very often, every once in a while the urge for fish strikes me.

On occasion, after a particularly good meal, I will look over at my wife and say "we eat good around here!" It has become a bit of a slogan for our wild game dinners, as well as for some of the other meals that we have that exceed our expectations. Even standard table fare such as beef and chicken can be a celebration of what God has given us, and pork ribs or beef brisket often cause me to utter this same slogan in reverence. Having access to the meat of so many of these wonderful game animals has been an incredible blessing in our lives, and I had to write about it here.

God clearly gives us permission to eat these things, as the verse from Acts at the beginning of this chapter shows us. In the verse, Peter was still looking at things from the point of view of the Law, and was not quite grasping the full impact of the New Covenant. He had become free to eat anything that God had blessed, and he was no longer under the requirements of Jewish Law.

While we too are free, we must remember that too much of a good thing can become a sin. Eat reasonable portions at mealtimes to avoid the sin of gluttony, and also be especially careful not to let game meats go to waste. It's our responsibility to show wisdom in the use of the things that we have been given, and our meals are no exception.

ACTION POINT: The next time you sit down to a venison dinner, be particularly thankful to God for the wild game meats that he has provided you. Avoid gluttony, but rejoice in the freedom that you have to eat so many different kinds of animals.

SURPRISED BY GOD

"And when he realized [this], he went to the house of Mary, the mother of John who was also called Mark, where many were gathered together and were praying. When he knocked at the door of the gate, a servant-girl named Rhoda came to answer. When she recognized Peter's voice, because of her joy she did not open the gate, but ran in and announced that Peter was standing in front of the gate. They said to her, 'You are out of your mind!' But she kept insisting that it was so. They kept saying, 'It is his angel.' But Peter continued knocking; and when they had opened [the door], they saw him and were amazed."

Acts 12:12-16

I went on my very first deer hunt during the Christmas holidays of 1985. Growing up on the outskirts of Charlotte, I had hunted small game like doves and squirrels many times before, but my first expedition for deer didn't happen until I was 18 years old. That first hunt was unsuccessful, and I would spend the next six years chasing deer before I finally got one.

From 1985 to 1991, I hunted the game lands of the Uwharrie National Forest near Albemarle, North Carolina. I hunted there with several different friends over the years, but none of us really knew what we were doing and we had no one to show us the right way to get a deer. It wasn't until late in 1991 that the situation changed for me.

My dad had a friend named Arnold who had been hunting deer and other big game for a great many years. Arnold had recently purchased 160 acres of land outside of Lancaster, South Carolina and had agreed to take me along on one of his hunts to help me get my first deer. It was to be a one-time deal, with Arnold doing this as a favor for my dad.

I gave Arnold a call and we worked out the details of the hunt. I would meet him at a gas station in Pineville on a Friday evening and then follow him from there down to his land. There was a camper on the property, and we would spend the night there along with his brother Gerald and a friend of theirs named Frank. This one hunt changed my life in a great many ways and led not only to my becoming a successful hunter, but it also ultimately brought my wife and I together when, many years later, Arnold introduced me to Gerald's daughter, whom I eventually married.

That's a story for another day, however, and today's topic is about being surprised by God. I did indeed meet up with Arnold and a few of his friends, and we all spent a cold Friday night in that little camper on his property. The next morning, Arnold told me how to get to a deer stand that he thought would be quite productive. He did caution me against shooting small bucks and said that he would prefer it if I were to just take a doe.

Leaving the camp, I made my way down the long trail to the climbing stand that Arnold had told me about, finally finding it attached to the base of a tall white oak tree several hundred yards from camp. I climbed up the tree as high as I could go, excited and ready for my first real chance at taking a deer.

I sat in that stand all morning, but the only thing I saw was a smallish spike buck. Remembering the rules that Arnold had laid down, I never even took the safety off of my rifle as I looked at the animal through my scope. He was indeed a young little deer, and would not have provided much in the way of venison. That was the first time that I ever saw a deer in the crosshairs of my rifle.

That was also the only deer that I saw that whole day, and though I hunted from a different stand that evening the deer just weren't moving. I was an incredibly frustrated young man as I made my way back to camp in the twilight of the evening. One chance to get a deer and I just couldn't make it happen. Arriving back at the trailer, I thanked Arnold for giving me the chance to hunt with him, and I began to load my gear into my truck.

"Why don't you come back and hunt with us again next weekend," Arnold asked as I closed the tailgate of my vehicle.

"You mean it?" I asked.

"Sure," he said. "I really want to see you get a deer."

My spirit soared as I drove back home that night. The following Friday evening after work I was back on the road to Lancaster, again full of hope that this would be the weekend that I would get my first deer. I would, I thought, do whatever it took to get me a deer this time.

The same guys were back in camp that evening, and as we sat around the camper talking Arnold told me about the stand that he wanted me to hunt from the next day. It was, he said, another climbing stand that sat on top of a long ridge that was full of white oaks. The acorns were on the ground, and the place ought to be full of deer. If I didn't see a deer there, he told me, then I was doing something wrong.

On Saturday morning we all headed out from the camp as we had the previous weekend. I followed a long trail of reflective tacks that led to the stand on the ridge, and upon finding it perched on the side of a white oak, I clambered aboard and ascended the tree. The view from the top of the oak was beautiful, and I just knew that I would see deer.

Four hours later I wasn't feeling quite so confident. Although those woods were such that you could just imagine them being full of deer, I hadn't seen a thing all morning; not even a squirrel. My frustration level reached its peak, and I actually even cried a little bit there in the tree. I had tried so hard for so many years to get a deer, and it seemed that it would never pay off. I looked at my watch and saw that it was 11:00am; far too late for deer to be moving.

I turned to God, as even the unbelievers among us will often do in moments like that. *God,* I prayed, *I have worked so hard to get a deer. I've spent hours and hours in the woods and haven't even come close to getting one. Would you help me? I don't want to go home empty handed yet again, and have to face all of my friends and tell them that I still haven't gotten a deer.*

That heartfelt prayer finished, I raised my head and opened my eyes. I started gathering my gear, ready to head down and hoping that my prayer would be answered for the evening hunt. Motion in the woods a hundred yards away caught my eye. Grabbing my binoculars, I focused them on the spot and saw three does feeding on acorns in a little clearing just down the trail from me.

I was absolutely amazed. I had asked a simple, genuine prayer, and God had answered it almost immediately. Although this was not the first time that He had answered a prayer of mine in an obvious way, I was astonished nonetheless. I thanked Him profusely with another very short prayer, and then gathered my wits about me.

I got my rifle up and centered the scope on one of the deer. I zoomed the scope in far enough to confirm that I as looking at a doe, and was glad to find that I was indeed looking at a female. Releasing the safety, I squeezed the trigger and watched as the little herd of animals scattered in three different directions. Scrambling down the tree with no concern for safety, I was on the ground and running within seconds of making the shot.

I ran over to where the deer had been standing and began looking for blood. I didn't immediately see anything, so I stopped and looked back toward the stand, wanting to be sure that I was in the right place. I was, so I again stared at the ground trying to find any sign of the deer, but didn't see anything at all. Dejected and disgusted, I wiped away another tear and stomped off toward camp.

The rest of the guys were already back at the camper when I got there. I told Arnold about missing the deer, and after asking me if I was *sure* that I had missed, he suggested that we take his dog Misty back into the woods to see if she could find any sign. That sounded like a good idea to me, so we whistled for the dog and went back into the woods.

Arriving back at the place where the deer had been standing, Misty almost immediately found a drop of blood that I had not seen. She bounded off into the woods, only to start barking a few minutes later.

She had found my deer lying in a patch of briars not fifty yards from where the deer had been standing. I think I probably cried a little bit again, but this time they were tears of relief as six years of fruitless deer hunting came to an end.

Why is it that we are so amazed when God comes through? He created the universe in seven days simply by speaking it into existence, so why do we get so astonished when He answers a simple prayer? We constantly show the same kind of disbelief that the disciples did when Peter was released from jail when instead we should be anticipating our prayers to be answered.

ACTION POINT: When you pray according to God's will, expect Him to come through. Don't be surprised when He does; He promises to provide for us, so take Him at his Word and be thankful for His generosity.

THE DOMINION OF MAN

"God blessed them; and God said to them, 'Be fruitful and multiply, and fill the earth, and subdue it; rule over the fish of the sea and over the birds of the sky and over every living thing that moves on the earth.'"

Genesis 1:28

I've been pretty fortunate in that in all of my years of hunting I've only had a few encounters with animal rights activists and anti-hunters. Most states have by now enacted laws that make it illegal to harass people who are engaged in legal outdoor activities, but my encounters came before these laws existed.

The first encounter that I had was extremely benign. My buddy Ted and I were up in Raleigh, North Carolina for the annual *Dixie Deer Classic*, which is a big hunting show that takes place in March of each year. Ted and I spent the day at the show, enjoying the exhibits and looking at all of the new gear that was going to be available for the coming season.

As the day wore on and the show drew to its close, we left the exhibit hall and headed out to the parking lot. As we walked to the truck, we saw a couple of guys dressed in animal suits holding signs that protested the show. We saw them again when we were driving out of the lot, and one of them – a guy dressed as a large rabbit – gave us a thumbs-down symbol and shook his sign at us as we left the lot.

My next meeting with anti-hunters had the potential to be a little bit more of a problem. Ted and I were hunting up in the Uwharrie National Forest on the opening day of deer season in the mid 90's this time around. We'd been hunting there for many years and had never had any problems before, but each year it seemed that more and more horseback riders were coming into the forest and riding the trails during the hunting seasons. I've got nothing against riding horses; I enjoy it myself on the rare occasions that I get a chance to do it. But this time they really showed their tails.

In Uwharrie, horseback riders are supposed to stay in a certain section of the forest that is closed to hunting. In this case, however, a group of riders had decided to ignore those rules and cut through the fields that we were hunting near. One of the riders, obviously half-drunk, saw Ted sitting in his tree stand on the edge of the field. The man stopped his horse, shot Ted a murderous look and shouted "Shoot me with an arrow, redneck." The girl with him, also drunk, yelled that we needed to give guns to the deer to make it fair.

Fortunately for everyone, after shouting those words they decided to leave the area, but our hunt was ruined for the day. Not only had their yelling scared off any deer that were in the area, but they had left me and Ted both fuming and unable to focus on the rest of the hunt. We left in disgust, and have only hunted in Uwharrie a couple of times since that day.

The perceived anonymity that the internet provides has given rise to a new form of false confidence, and it is through this venue that I have had my most recent encounters with these misguided people. For the past ten years I've kept detailed journals of all of my hunts online on my personal website. They are available for anyone to peruse, and in recent years I have even opened up a forum to allow people to comment on my hunts.

While the vast majority of the comments that I have received had been positive, there are some that have been quite abusive in their tone and content. I have been insulted, threatened, and cursed at more times than I care to count. People have suggested that all hunters should be killed, and they express joy when an article on my site mentions any kind of hunting accident that has occurred anywhere in America. It's amazingly hypocritical of these anti-hunters to wish death upon humans while condemning the killing of animals.

It's also completely unbiblical. In Genesis, God clearly gives man authority over all of the fish and animals of the world. With that authority comes the responsibility to exercise good stewardship over what God has given us, and sound conservation practices are part of that stewardship. Science has proven that hunting is a key part of conservation, but anti-hunters will not accept this fact. They often will not accept the authority given to us by the Bible either, which makes us doubly disadvantaged when we try to reason with them.

Ultimately, however, we do have the advantage, because the truth is on our side. When the facts are carefully examined, animal rights activists and anti-hunters are in the wrong. They are wrong from a scientific point of view, and they are wrong from a Biblical point of view. Remember that when dealing with them, but also remember not to let them cause you to escalate during any confrontations that you may have with them.

ACTION POINT: Take time to learn about how hunting plays a key role in conservation. Be prepared to back your arguments with facts when dealing with anti-hunters and animal rights activists. Also remember that you are representing all of us when you are confronted by them, and act accordingly. Ask God to be your strength and your shield during any of these confrontations that may arise.

THE OCTOBER FAWN

"Then the LORD took note of Sarah as He had said, and the LORD did for Sarah as He had promised. So Sarah conceived and bore a son to Abraham in his old age, at the appointed time of which God had spoken to him."

Genesis 21:1-2

In the chapter entitled *The Importance of Sound Doctrine*, I talked about some of the myths associated with deer hunting. There are many things that we read and hear about deer that simply aren't true, and the astute hunter will take the time to study his quarry in the wild if he truly wants to learn about deer.

For example, it's common knowledge among hunters that the peak of deer breeding activity, which is known as "the rut", takes place anywhere from early October to late November depending on what part of the country you hunt in. Most hunters are also aware that a second round of breeding can occur a month later, when does that were not impregnated during the true rut come back into fertility.

However, God works in many ways, and in this world that He has created not everything happens according to a set schedule. Back in 2008, I was deer hunting on Halloween down in Kershaw Country, South Carolina. As I was driving down one of the logging roads on my lease, I saw a small deer standing at the edge of the woods just ahead of me.

I gunned the engine, wanting to get a look at the deer. As I drew close, I could see that it was a very tiny deer indeed. It turned out that it was a spotted fawn, and from the size of it, it couldn't have been more than a week or two old. It was tiny and looked as if it had just started traveling around with its mother.

When born, fawns tend to stay in one place for the first couple of weeks, as they are extremely small and vulnerable to predation at this time. They don't really begin moving around until they reach the end of their first month of life, at which time they'll begin following their mother around and learning about what it means to be a deer. Whitetail deer have a two hundred day gestational period, and given the extra month in which it would have stayed in one place, my estimation put the breeding date for the fawn's mother at around March 15th of that year.

Even making the estimate of the fawn's age very conservative and saying that it was two months old when I saw it would put the breeding date in the middle of February. I've seen a lot of deer in my time, and have studied their behavior in both the woods and in my own back yard, and I'm positive that this was a month old fawn.

Setting the math and the calculations aside, I remember looking at this little fawn in amazement. It was like a gift from God to be seeing such a beautiful young animal with the brilliantly colored leaves still on the trees, and with the chill of November in the air. Seeing the fawn caused me to stop and think about how God is not bound by the rules of man. This little fawn, conceived many months after the traditional rut, showed me the Hand of God in a powerful way that morning.

ACTION POINT: When was the last time that you were amazed at something that you saw in God's creation? The October fawn reminded me of the majesty of God, but even more so it reminded me of His sovereignty. Keep in mind that God is in control, and if He could give Sarah a child at 99 years old, He can make deer that breed outside of the bounds of the rut.

GIRL CRAZY

"For the lips of an adulteress drip honey and smoother than oil is her speech; but in the end she is bitter as wormwood, sharp as a two-edged sword. Her feet go down to death, her steps take hold of Sheol. She does not ponder the path of life; her ways are unstable, she does not know [it]. Now then, [my] sons, listen to me and do not depart from the words of my mouth. Keep your way far from her and do not go near the door of her house."

Proverbs 5:3-8

At some point in every boy's life, his thoughts will begin to turn to the opposite sex. It varies from boy to boy as to how old he is when this happens, but it's as natural a thing as rain from the sky. Once he's started down that path and has seen the beauty of a woman, he's hooked for life. The tough part as a parent is steering him in the right direction and giving him the proper focus for that energy.

It happens to animals too, but in different ways. Female deer, for example, become fertile in the late fall of the year, and when this happens the bucks go girl crazy. Deer hunters look forward to the rut with great enthusiasm, but I can assure you that the bucks themselves look forward to it even more. I've seen wise old swamp donkeys lose their wits in the presence of a doe that has come into estrus, and such foolishness has cost them their lives.

I remember one time when I was hunting a long power line right-of-way down in Lancaster, South Carolina. It was late October, and the rut was in full swing. A group of does was feeding in a wheat field that was in the middle of the right-of-way, when suddenly a pretty nice eight point buck leapt out of the woods and landed right in the middle of the does.

I was watching this through my binoculars, and I swear that his tongue was hanging out of his mouth as he jumped this way and that, unable to decide which doe to chase. He had a big sloppy grin on his face, and to this day I have never seen a deer that was wearing a more human expression. He chased the does in circles around the field, running left and right, back and forth. I put a stop to the silliness with a round from my 7mm magnum, and the does scattered as the buck collapsed in a heap, dead where he stood.

Now, we know that deer are designed to act this way. When a buck smells the urine from a doe that is ready to be bred, he'll follow her trail until he finds her. He'll quit paying attention to the world around him and will focus on the doe, and nothing will get in the way of his single-minded quest. This is the way that God made deer, but as humans we are supposed to know better.

We males certainly don't seem to know better though, and I'm appalled at the things that I see on television and hear on the radio. Every show that I turn on portrays men as idiots and women as oversexed vixens who will do anything for a date. It seems like the rut is not only going on in the deer woods, but also in modern culture. This is why there is not a single modern sitcom that I watch, and it's also why I only rarely go to the movies.

I'm looking at this from the front end of things, with my first child due to be born in the next couple of months. But as a father, I want to teach him the wisdom that I've learned in my forty-some years, and help him to learn to pursue a woman the way God designed men to do. It's a difficult path to walk on, but fortunately it's still a few years before I have to start really thinking about it.

But as my son grows, I'll be pointing him to the passages in the Bible that deal with men and women, teaching him the Lord's way from a very young age. We're already praying for his future wife, that she will be raised in a Godly family and that she will come to know Him and live by His precepts. We're praying too that she will remain pure and not give in to the pressures of modern society and the sexualization of young women that is occurring these days.

We're praying for his friends too, asking that God will put him in the company of young men who are being raised in like manner. It's not too early to be thinking about these things, and I look forward to seeing how God will answer these prayers. He knows better than any of us how tough things are in this modern world, and how much pressure there is on teenagers to give in to sexual temptation.

We'll keep on praying both for my son Paul and for the girl who will eventually become his wife. I'm hoping that by the time he's old enough to chase women, he won't act like the bucks that I've watched year after year in the deer woods. I'm hoping that he chooses wisdom and does it God's way.

ACTION POINT: Watch how the bucks act during the rut this year. Compare that to your own history with women. Have you chased them in wisdom or in foolishness? What does the Bible say about this kind of behavior?

SHOOT STRAIGHT

"But above all, my brethren, do not swear, either by heaven or by earth or with any other oath; but your yes is to be yes, and your no, no, so that you may not fall under judgment."

James 5:12

In most of my early hunting experiences where I took friends along with me, we never had anything "cool" to say to each other before entering the woods. Usually we'd just exchange a quick "good luck" as we went our separate ways to our stands. It actually occurred to me at some point to try to come up with something to say that would sound good, but nothing ever really came to mind that worked well.

That changed the first time I took a veteran deer hunter with me on one of my hunts up on the Uwharrie game lands. I was just out of college and was living at my parent's house at the time, and the neighboring house was rented by four guys in their late twenties or early thirties. They were all from Pennsylvania, and one of them had killed a great many deer up there in his years in the woods. Steve was his name.

When he learned that I was a hunter, Steve expressed interest in going with me and trying to help me get my first deer. The first time we hunted together was on a snowy December day in around 1990. Riding up to the game lands in my truck, Steve gave me a few pointers about hunting deer in the snow. I was excited about the hunt, and couldn't wait to get into the woods.

Once we had parked the truck at my favorite hunting spot, I pointed out where I'd be heading. Steve took a look around and decided to do some still hunting, making a long circle by following an old creek bed around the base of the small mountain where I'd be hunting. As we parted, Steve whispered to me, "Good luck buddy. Shoot straight."

As he walked away, I grinned. I knew that this was a saying that I'd be using in the future with other hunters. Shoot straight. I liked the way that it sounded, as well as the implication that there would actually be something to shoot at. I filed this away for future use, then turned and went on into the woods myself.

Neither Steve nor I got a deer that day. I really don't remember much about the hunt itself, but I do know that we came home empty handed. Steve hunted with me several more times over the course of that season, and although we never did get a deer I remember that his parting words were always the same: shoot straight. I also remember that I tried it out on my buddy Ted a couple of times when we were hunting together, and it wasn't long before he was saying it himself.

Now that I'm older I'm not concerned with having a cool thing to say to my buddies when we hunt together. However, I'm still drawn to that little expression, but these days it's for a different reason. I see a second meaning in it now that I never saw in the past. There's the obvious message that says that your bullet or arrow should fly true to its target, but the deeper meaning is that we should be tellers of the truth whenever we speak; that whatever we say should be accurate and direct.

For most of my life I avoided straight talk. When asked where I wanted to go out to eat, for example, if I was among a group of guys I would give a non-answer such as "anything is fine with me." When asked to do almost anything at work, I would say "yes sir" and get the job done, regardless of whether or not I had a differing opinion about what actually needed to be done. It wasn't until recent years that I even realized that I was doing this, and the passage from James above helped me to take a new direction in how I communicate with people.

If asked where I want to eat, I will now say so directly and without worrying about what the other guys think of my choice. If they don't like what I've picked, I'm more than happy to negotiate and go somewhere else, but I expect the people around me to tell me when they don't like the choice that I've made.

At work, I am more vocal about the tasks that I am given. If a job is assigned to me that does not seem to be the best approach to a problem, I'll give my opinion and suggest that we take a different path. If something can't be done in the given timeframe, I will let my boss know and give him a realistic estimate of when it can be done. I'm not saying that I reject work or that I respond in an inappropriate way, but I do make sure that I provide my recommendations when necessary. That's part of what they're paying me for.

Another choice that I've made in shooting straight is that when I am around an indecisive person, I will not pander to that indecision, but will instead be very direct and make choices where needed. If someone says "it doesn't matter where we eat," then I will step forward and make the choice. And again, I am not doing this in a tactless way or in a manner that makes the other person look or feel bad, but I have decided that I will not be an indecisive man.

I think this is pretty much what Scripture is telling us to do. In the first chapter of James, he talks about indecisive men as being like ships being tossed back and forth on the waves of an angry sea. I don't want to be that kind of man. I've decided that I will "shoot straight" not only in the deer woods, but also with my words and deeds. I think James would approve.

> **ACTION POINT:** In what ways do you need to work on "shooting straight" when dealing with others? Have you made the decision to let your "yes" be yes and your "no" be no? If not, what does God say about that kind of communication pattern?

PLAYING BY THE RULES

"Also if anyone competes as an athlete, he does not win the prize unless he competes according to the rules."

2 Timothy 2:5

Hunters, like any other people who participate in activities that are regulated by law, have a core choice to make when it comes to how they pursue their pastime. The key thing that a hunter has to decide upon is whether he will or won't he play by the rules. Most states have a large number of laws that govern how hunting must be done, and the hunter must choose whether he will follow these laws or ignore them.

Often, the rules may seem silly upon close inspection. For example, why is it that in some states archery equipment may not be used during the gun deer season? Why is it illegal to hunt on Sundays in states like Maine and Virginia? Why do different counties have different rules when it comes to baiting deer? The South Carolina regulations guide is the size of a small magazine, and each year I always have to spend several hours familiarizing myself with the new laws.

As a hunter, I've had many chances to choose whether or not to follow the game laws, in both little ways and much bigger ones. The first time that comes to mind happened on my very first "real" deer hunt on private lands. By the late 1980's, I'd been on lots of hunts on game lands, but had never had the chance to hunt on private land. That changed in around 1987.

In that year, the home next door to my parent's house was purchased by a family from Fayetteville, NC. The family had been cotton farmers down in eastern North Carolina, but when a tractor accidently left the father of the family permanently disabled, they left the farm and moved up to Charlotte. They kept the land in the family, and in September their son, Bobby, invited me to go down and do a little bit of deer hunting on their property. I couldn't resist the invitation.

Late one Friday afternoon we packed up my truck and made the two and a half hour drive down to their farm. Although we were going to be staying at his grandmother's house, when we got to Fayetteville Bobby suggested that we first drive out to the fields to get a look at where we'd be hunting the next day. With him navigating, we had soon left the paved road and were driving through the soft sandy roads that covered the farm.

As we turned into a particularly large field, my headlights splashed against the wood-line two hundred yards away and we could see a herd of deer standing there feeding. Before I knew it, Bobby had jumped out of the truck, uncased his rifle, and was about to take a shot at the deer.

"What the heck are you doing?" I yelled, turning off my lights. I actually used some stronger language there, but for now we'll just go with "heck".

"Turn the headlights back on," he yelled back. "I can get one of those deer from here!"

"Are you crazy?" I replied. "I didn't come down here to get arrested for spotlighting deer."

"There's not a game warden for miles around here," Bobby said. "I don't know what your problem is."

"Put the rifle up, or we're heading home. I'm not going to do this," I told him.

"Fine," he huffed. "I wouldn't have asked you down here if I had known you were going to be this way."

There was a good bit of tension between us as he put his rifle back in the case. He shook his head, muttering about missing the opportunity to make an easy shot at a deer. We didn't talk about the incident again on the trip, and instead we let the silence ease the tension. We went ahead and hunted the next day, but neither of us saw anything. That was also the last time we ever hunted together.

In the chapter called *Temptation*, I told you about the time that the bobcat came out in front of my deer stand and sat there not ten yards away from me for quite some time. The chances that I would have gotten caught shooting that bobcat out of season were very low, but I knew that I would never be able to look at his mounted body and feel good about it if I had taken him out of season.

I talked to a taxidermist friend of mine about it later, and he told me that in the twenty years that he'd been in that field, never once had a game warden questioned him about the legality of any of the predators that were brought into his shop. Not so with deer, but with the smaller game they didn't really seem to care. Even so, I still maintain that I would not be able to look at an illegal animal on my wall and feel even slightly good about it.

By its very nature, hunting takes you away from the public eye while you are afield, and often you yourself are the only witness to the choices that you make in the woods. Whether it's taking a shot at an animal that is not quite in season or a much larger violation like spotlighting deer or shooting a doe when it's not an either sex day, there are so many chances to break the rules that the Christian sportsman must really watch himself carefully to ensure that he stays within the bounds of the law.

They say that character is what you do when no one is watching, and a hunter who obeys all of the game laws when he is alone in the woods is indeed a man of good character. It's obviously important to God that we following the game laws; Paul tells us in Romans 13 that we are to be subject to the governing authorities, and since it is the government that sets the game laws we must obey them.

Scripture makes it clear that the only time we are free to break the laws of man is when those laws conflict with our obedience to God and what He has commanded of us. There's a story that's told in Acts that illustrates this. In verse 5:29, Peter was standing before the high priest, having been arrested for preaching and teaching in the name of Christ.

The priest tells Peter that he had warned him about doing this, and he is questioning Peter about his continued disobedience to the orders of the temple leaders. Peter responds by saying that he must obey what God has asked of him, not the orders of men.

In hunting, we have no mandate from God as to *how* we are to exercise our dominion over the animals. Therefore we must follow the laws that our fish and game departments have set for us, since they are not in conflict with God's law. If all hunting were abolished as some misguided animal rights activists desire it to be, then there might indeed be some conflict with what God has told us about having good stewardship over what we have been given, and I doubt that I myself would ever stop hunting altogether.

> **ACTION POINT:** What does your decision about whether or not to obey hunting laws say about your character? Think about that the next time you are faced with temptation in the woods.

WEAPON SAFETY

"Train up a child in the way he should go, even when he is old he will not depart from it."

Proverbs 22:6

As anyone who has been around guns and hunting long enough knows, learning to be safe with your weapons is critically important both for you and for those that you hunt with. I've been pretty lucky in my almost thirty years afield in that I've never had any kind of accident with my weapons, nor have I been present when someone else has.

My dad introduced us to guns at a fairly early age; we used to shoot his little .22 in the woods across the street from our house once in a while, and we were given BB guns when we were still pretty young. He even gave me a 20 gauge shotgun in my early teenage years, and it's my intention to pass that same gun on to my own son when he is old enough. I will give that gun to him only after he has been exposed to gun safety rules to such a degree that they are ingrained in him.

Although his object lessons were unintentional, the things that my dad taught us about guns have stayed with me all of my life. There are two lessons in particular that stand out in my mind, and although he didn't mean for them to happen the way that they did, I believe that the results of those two lessons have remained fresh in my mind because of the unexpected way that they ended up.

Our first BB gun was a little lever action Daisy "99 Champion", a straight shooting little cowboy style rifle that had a really nice look and feel. Shortly after he bought the gun for us, he explained to us that we must always make sure that the lever was fully returned to the closed position prior to firing the weapon. If we tried to shoot the gun with the level open, it would slam shut and would likely bruise our hand or even cut off a couple of fingers.

He decided to demonstrate this for us. Cocking the rifle, he left the lever in the open position and then looked around the yard for something to pull the trigger with. He found a broken branch from a pine tree in the side yard that looked like it would work, and then told us to watch carefully. He then proceeded to pull the trigger using the branch, and the lever did indeed slam closed as quickly and as powerfully as he said it would.

Unfortunately, it turned out that the stick was a little bit stronger than the metal of the lever on the rifle, and instead of breaking the stick the lever itself broke off, rendering the little air rifle useless. We were young enough that I think my brother and I both started crying, seeing that our new BB gun was out of commission. The object lesson stuck with us though, and to this day I have never fired a lever action rifle of any kind with the lever in the open position.

I remember writing a letter to Daisy asking them to send us a new lever for the rifle. I didn't know the word "action" at the time, and I believe I called it a "cocker" in the note, but they responded quickly and before long our little gun was back in commission. It wasn't long after that that my dad decided to give us our second lesson in gun safety.

Our entire family was sitting in the den one day when my dad started talking about guns. We must always, he said, treat a gun as if it were loaded. Guns load themselves, he told us, and if we acted as if each one that we touched was loaded we would never accidentally hurt anyone with it. I'm not sure why he did this, but he got the BB gun out from its hiding place, cocked it, and then dry fired it at the den window.

As you can probably imagine, the gun had apparently indeed loaded itself, because the next thing we knew there was a tinkle of glass as one of the panes in the window shattered. And so there was my second object lesson; never fire a gun in the house or you might raise the ire of your wife as she sees that her den suddenly needs a new window. Like the previous lesson, this one stuck with me as well, and I have never fired so much as a BB gun in the house even knowing that it is empty.

Although the birth of my son is still a couple of months away as I write this, I am already thinking about the things that I will teach him regarding guns. Since I am a hunter, a gun owner, and a concealed carry advocate, he will be around guns from a very early age. I am hoping that he will develop the same kind of interest in them that I have, and that we will be able to enjoy many father/son days both in the woods and at the rifle range.

However, I am fully aware that he may not be interested in things like hunting, guns, and the outdoors. Whether he chooses to participate in these activities later on in life or not, he'll be schooled in them as soon as he is old enough to understand them. If he decides not to own guns once he grows up and leaves our house, he will at least make this choice from an informed position.

In the same way, he will be taught Scripture from a very early age. The Bible tells us that we are to constantly teach our children about God, and to bring Him up at every opportunity. My wife and I are committed to making sure that our son is shown the way to live a Godly life, and to walk with Him in all that he does. We can only pray that he will remember the things that we have taught him and that he will make decisions based on what he has learned from us. In these ways, we will honor both him and God.

ACTION POINT: Do you practice gun safety at all times, but even more diligently when in the presence of your children? What are you teaching them whenever you are afield with a weapon in hand? Likewise, what does the way you live your life say to them about your relationship with God? Remember always that they are watching everything that you do and say.

ANSWERED PRAYERS

"This is the confidence which we have before Him, that if we ask anything according to His will, He hears us. And if we know that He hears us [in] whatever we ask, we know that we have the requests which we have asked from Him."

1 John 5:14-15

I've already talked about the way God answers our prayers in the chapter called *Surprised by God*, but something happened to me recently that made me want to write about it again. I've also talked several times about the upcoming birth of my son, and this experience that I just had ties into that as well.

Each year as deer season approaches, I start talking to my boss at work about taking some time off to hunt. I've been quite lucky throughout the course of my entire career; every manager that I've worked for has realized how important hunting is to me, and without fail they have allowed me to take off lots of time during the season. I use almost all of my vacation time in the last four months of the year, and I have spent an average of thirty days in the woods each year for the last dozen deer seasons.

This year, however, our son is due to be born during the first week of November, right around the peak of the rut in my part of South Carolina, and right in the prime of the hunting season. My days afield will be limited this year, and although I hope to get a few afternoon hunts in during late November and early December, I doubt that I'll get many full days in the woods once October arrives.

To that end, I have been praying hard about the hunting that I'll do this season. Even before the season began, I was asking God to help me get a really good buck this year. I've taken a great many eight point bucks over the last twenty –five seasons, and I've passed on at least one nine pointer, but this year I really wanted something better than an eight.

I didn't realize it, but my wife was praying that for me as well. So it was no surprise to her that on the opening day of the 2010 season, I called her from the road as I was leaving the woods and heading back home. I was calling to explain to her why I was running so late, and that the reason was that I had gotten the deer of my dreams. But I'm getting ahead of myself; let me back up and tell the story from the beginning.

A couple of years back I got interested in trail cameras. I'll talk more about them another time, but for now suffice to say that I've bought three of them over the course of the last two years, and now one of my favorite hobbies is moving them around to different spots on my deer lease and driving down each weekend to see what I've captured. I did this over the entire summer of 2010, and continued doing it as deer season opened at the first of September.

By the time that archery season arrived, I had found a great location for one of my cameras and was regularly getting a really nice eight point buck on film. Once, however, I had gotten a snapshot of a ten pointer, and he quickly became the focus of my hunts. He only showed up on camera one time, but over the course of four bow hunts I sat in the tree hoping to see him. Not only did I not see him, but I actually didn't see a single deer during any of my hunts.

Although it was frustrating not to see any deer, my camera was showing me that they were constantly moving through the area that I had chosen to hunt in, and if I sat there long enough I would certainly see deer. I may not see my ten pointer, or even the big eight that I had gotten on camera, but at least I would see some does. I remained committed to hunting in the box blind that was near my camera until I saw a deer.

On the opening day of the 2010 rifle deer season, I arrived at the lease a bit early, wanting to be the first one at our sign-in board so that I could be sure to get the spot I wanted. When I pulled up to the board, I saw that four other guys were already there, but fortunately none of them had chosen my spot. After greeting them and wishing them all good luck, I drove on up the logging road and headed into the woods.

After parking my Jeep about a quarter of a mile away from the stand, I made my way quietly up the trail and got into the box blind without making too much noise. It was still pitch dark, so I settled in and got comfortable, knowing that I had a long wait in front of me before daylight arrived. When dawn finally started to break, I sat up straighter in my seat and shook myself out of the light doze that I had fallen into.

I sat quietly in the stand for four and a half hours, diligently scanning the woods to the left and to the right of the blind. Only a few turkeys crossed the trail from time to time; never once did I see a deer. The sun was shining brightly on the blind, and it was quickly becoming unbearably hot. I knew that I wouldn't be able to sit still much longer.

At 10:30, I had had enough of the heat and knew that I needed a break. I left the stand and walked down to my camera with a new memory card in hand. I pulled the used card from the camera and replaced it with the empty one, and then walked back to the stand, gathered my gear, and hiked back to the Jeep. When I got there, I started the truck and turned on the air conditioner, then transferred the pictures from the card to my iPad.

There were well over a thousand pictures on the card, which surprised me since I had just changed it out not four days earlier. As I looked through the pictures, I sat up straight in my seat in surprise. Apparently, in the early hours of the morning just before I had gotten in the stand, a buck with at least eleven points had visited my camera. Looking farther back through the pictures, I also saw that a really big eight pointer had shown up in broad daylight on the previous afternoon. Further, a group of five or six does were visiting the area every day shortly after noon.

Seeing that all of those deer were visiting my stand pretty regularly, I was in a hurry to get back in the blind, but first I needed a small bit of lunch to energize me for the rest of the day. I drove out of the lease and tagged out, meeting fellow club member Phil Pike at the sign-in board. Phil told me that he would be spending that afternoon hunting in a stand not far from mine, and that if I shot a deer I was welcome to come and get him to help retrieve it. I thanked him and headed into town for a sandwich.

When I got back to the lease, I parked my truck in the same place that I had left it earlier that morning, and then made my way up the road to the stand. It was around 11:30 when I got back into the blind. My camera had shown me that deer were coming in at 12:30 each day, so I quickly settled into place and began my wait.

Five hours later I was still waiting. No deer had appeared, and I was sweating profusely and only had about two or three swallows of water left in my bottle. Wiping the sweat from my brow, I shifted positions and continued watching the trail. As I watched, a deer finally showed up. I raised my binoculars and saw that it was a buck, and being on the verge of dehydration I decided to take the shot and end the hunt. He looked to be an eight pointer, and I could see that he was a shooter. Getting my rifle into position, I squeezed the trigger and watched as the buck jerked and then ran off into the woods.

I quickly left my blind and went back to my Jeep; I wanted to have it close by so that it would be available when I retrieved the deer. Walking down the road, I saw Phil coming my way in the distance. He had heard the shot and was coming to offer assistance in finding the deer. I thanked him for his help and told him that the deer had indeed run off into the woods and that we would need to track it.

We found a bit of blood in the dirt where the deer had been standing, but did not see any more no matter how hard we looked. We did see several scuff marks in the pine needles where the deer had run, so Phil and I split up, each taking a different angle down into the swamp trying to find where it had gone. When we met up again Phil told me that he had been walking on the edge of a thicket when he jumped my buck. It was wounded, he said, but he could not tell how badly.

We backed out of the woods and decided to wait thirty or forty-five minutes before pushing the buck any harder. Those of you who have been in a situation like this know how difficult of a wait it can be when you've got a wounded animal in the bush and you are anxious to get on the trail, but you know that it is best to give him some time before you do. As we left the woods, I prayed hard that we would find my buck.

When it was time to get back on the trail, we quickly found the spot where the deer had been bedded down. There was bright red blood there in the thicket, which greatly encouraged me. We followed the trail of blood for a dozen yards, but it quickly gave out. Continuing on, we soon jumped him again about a hundred yards from where he had first laid down.

Normally in a situation like this I would back off and return the next day, but several things were working against us. First, it was still very hot this time of year, and the meat would spoil if left over night. Second, the coyotes or a bear would probably get to the deer before we did, and lastly, I had to work the next morning and could not take the day off. Knowing that, we decided to push on and try to tire the buck out. I offered up another brief prayer asking that we would find this deer, and then we were off.

We tracked that deer for a quarter of a mile through the swamp. Twice more we jumped him, and twice more we lost sight of him. Finally, as I walked down to a creek bed to see if I could find any tracks where he might have crossed, I looked to my left and saw him sitting there in the dry creek looking at me. I quickly raised my rifle and delivered the finishing shot, and then ran over to look at him. It turned out not to be an eight pointer at all; the deer had a full eleven points on his rack, the most points of any deer that I've ever taken. I collapsed on the ground in joy and exhaustion.

My dehydration was getting the best of me, and although I helped a bit at first I had to rely on Phil to do most of the work as we dragged the deer out of the swamp. I had to stop and rest several times on the way out of the woods, and I repeatedly chastised myself for not bringing enough water into the stand with me on a day as hot as this one had been.

Knowing that my friend Arnold was also hunting at the lease that night and that he had brought his Polaris Ranger UTV with him, we left the buck lying in a grassy area in the woods several hundred yards from the stand. Using Arnold's vehicle we were able to drive down to where he left the buck, load him into the buggy, and then carry him the rest of the way out of the woods in a much easier manner.

When we got him back to the truck, I again offered a prayer; this time one of thanks. I thanked God for allowing me to shoot an eleven point buck and also that Phil and Arnold were there to help. This deer truly was an answered prayer. I had desperately wanted something better than an eight this year, and God had delivered it in a powerful way. When I called my wife to tell here about the deer, she told me that she too had been praying that this would be the year that I got a ten pointer or better.

God answered those prayers. Too many things worked out "just right" that day for it to be anything other than His hand upon my hunt. Though I may not take another buck this season, or even a doe, I will remember this year as including one of the best hunts of my life as I scored big on that September evening in the deer woods. I will also remember the way that God answered the prayers of both myself and my wife.

> **ACTION POINT:** God is faithful to answer our prayers when they are in accordance with His will. I was not asking for a world record buck; only one better than I had shot in previous years. If you have a specific goal in your hunting, don't hesitate to ask God to help you achieve it.

HOW MUCH HOTTER THE FIRES OF HELL

"But for the cowardly and unbelieving and abominable and murderers and immoral persons and sorcerers and idolaters and all liars, their part [will be] in the lake that burns with fire and brimstone, which is the second death."

Revelation 21:8

Although I've already taken the best whitetail of my life this year, the early part of the 2010 deer season has been a very difficult one for me. It just seems like it's been a lot hotter this year that it usually is. I don't buy into the global warming nonsense; at least not into the theory that man has caused it, but I will say that the first part of this season has been quite a bit more uncomfortable than normal. As I write this chapter, it is early in October, and only now are the temperatures starting to drop.

In South Carolina our deer season opens on two different dates, depending on where you will be hunting. In the lowcountry it starts in mid-August, which is absolutely amazing to me. How anyone can sit in a tree on the fifteenth of August is beyond me, yet when the season opens two weeks later in my part of the state there I am high in a tree drenched with sweat and surrounded with mosquitoes. It doesn't make sense to go afield in weather like this, and yet we do it year after year.

For the last ten years or so I have kept detailed journal entries for every hunt that I have taken. Although I quit keeping track of the temperature for each hunt back in 2009, in writing this chapter I looked at my records from before that and saw that it has indeed been an average of fifteen degrees hotter on deer hunting days this year. Twice during hunts this year I have stripped down to nothing but shorts as I've sat in deer blinds where the temperatures have exceeded one hundred degrees. I've even found myself at the point of dehydration after leaving my stand on at least two evenings this year.

One of the other club members and I were discussing the heat on the phone the other day. On his last hunt, this fellow had chosen a ladder stand that unfortunately faced directly into the sun. By the time the hunt was over he too was seriously dehydrated and had gotten a pretty good sunburn, which is at least a little bit unusual for this time of year. We talked about how we are both actually feeling a bit of dread at the thought of getting back into our stands in this heat. It's just not right!

Switching gears a bit, you've probably figured out by now that I am, for the most part, a fundamentalist Christian, however, I've always felt that my calling is to see sportsmen grow in Christ rather than to bring the lost to Him. The Great Commission in Matthew 28:16-20 does indeed tell us to take the message of Christ to a lost and dying world, and I do believe that all of us who are saved have a duty to do exactly that. I've never been very good at witnessing, but I agree that it is a powerful tool in bringing others to Christ.

However, my heart does not break for the lost the way that the hearts of many other Christians do. I surely desire salvation for those who do not yet know Christ, but I have not felt a great passion for taking the Gospel to those people. Instead, my heart is geared toward helping hunters move forward in their Christian walk, teaching them to live a more Godly life even as I myself learn to do so.

Even knowing that this is my focus, as I sat sweating in the sweltering heat of my box blind on opening day of the deer season this year, I couldn't help but think that no matter how hot I was, the fires of hell are going to be much hotter for those who do not accept Christ. On that particular day I did indeed feel a great sadness for the lost as I sat in my stand I thought about the unending fires of hell; a real place in which a great many souls will spend eternity.

It was unusual for me to be thinking of things like this, and yet I can't help but feel that God was putting this matter on my heart so that I could write about it in this book. The thoughts of hell weighed so heavily upon me that I knew that I had to write at least one chapter about it. For the fires of hell are indeed immeasurably hotter than what I endured in the deer stand on that summer afternoon, and I do not want to see even one of my fellow sportsmen, friends, or family members have to face that kind of eternity.

ACTION POINT: Although my writings are typically directed at those who already know Christ as Lord and Savior, I'd like to pause here and address my readers who are not yet Christians. I urge you, friends, to read the Gospel of John and then accept Christ into your heart. Heed the calling of the Holy Spirit and join us in eternal salvation.

TAKING CARE OF YOUR EQUIPMENT

"His master said to him, 'Well done, good and faithful slave. You were faithful with a few things, I will put you in charge of many things; enter into the joy of your master.'"

Matthew 25:21

In that last year or so, I've realized that I have reached the point in my life where the equipment that I use for hunting today is, for the most part, the same equipment that I will be using for the rest of my life. I've gone through several different pairs of binoculars in the last thirty years, and have upgraded my bow twice in that time. I've used a variety of scopes on my rifles, and indeed have used several different guns as my primary hunting weapon over the years. Deer, duck, and turkey calls have come and gone, as have seat cushions, rifle rests, and other gear.

As I enter middle age, I'm finding that I'm now quite comfortable with the things that I own. I've had my latest pair of binoculars for about eight years now, and as I finally have some quality optics there is no reason for me to replace them in the future. I'm very happy with the way that my Remington 7mm magnum shoots, and I'm extremely pleased with the scope that I have chosen for it. Indeed, I've been wearing the same pair of snake boots for ten hunting seasons now, and they are showing no real sign of wear.

I've gotten a bit addicted to high-powered flashlights in the last few years, and I now have a primary and a backup unit that will also probably last for the rest of my life. Both of them are amazingly bright to be as small as they are, and I'm very careful to put them in a safe place each time I get home from hunting.

One of the reasons that my things are lasting longer is that I have finally learned how to take proper care of them. For many years I did not treat my things the way I should have, with my guns left uncleaned at the end of the hunting season and my deer hunting gear scattered over a wide variety of places in my house, garage and workshop. When deer season rolled around, I often could not find half of the things that I wanted to take into the stand with me simply because I had no idea what I had done with them on the last occasion that I used them.

A couple of years ago I got tired of having to buy new stuff every year, so I went out and got some of the new-fangled garage organizers; those tracks that you screw into your wall and then hang hooks off of. On one side of the garage all of my tree stands are now hanging neatly from the wall, and on the other I have my backpacks, callers, tubs full of my hunting clothes, and a wooden boot rack that I built and varnished a few years back.

This system has worked extremely well for me. On the day before any of my hunts, I am now organized enough that I can load my truck in mere minutes without having to worry about whether or not I've left something behind. When I come home at the end of a hunt, I always put things back in their proper place before I even step into the house. My boots go right back on the rack, my backpack hangs from its hook, and my drink cooler goes up on the shelf beside my truck.

If I leave something behind nowadays, it usually happens at the change of a season; bow to rifle, deer to duck or duck to turkey, and not because I don't know where I left my equipment. It took me twenty-five years of hunting to reach this point, but now that I'm here I feel like it's the right place to be. I've gone from pack rat to borderline neat-freak, but at least I know where my stuff is nowadays.

Until recently, I've wondered what would become of all of my hunting gear and my animal heads after I'm gone. As I've mentioned several times before, we now have a son on the way, and I'm hoping that he will treasure the guns, bows, and other equipment that I plan to leave for him. I'd like to think that he'll enjoy having my mounts to look at one day, and my guns to hunt with and to pass on to his own children. It may not work out that way, but that at least is my dream.

Even so, the Bible makes it clear that we are not the real owner of our things; God is. Everything belongs to Him, and we are only the temporary custodians. For that reason alone, we should practice good stewardship over the things that have been entrusted to us. That goes for our guns, our hunting clothes, and all of our gear, not to mention our homes and vehicles. By doing right with the things that He has given us, how much more will we be given in the kingdom of heaven?

I've always been fascinated with the parable of the talents. Three men are each entrusted with a bit of money while their master is away. When he returns, he asks what they have done with it. Two of the men had invested their money and had increased the amount that they had. The third man had hidden his away, knowing that his master was a hard man. The third man is denied a place in the kingdom for his action. This shows us how we too must be wise with the things that God has entrusted us with.

ACTION POINT: How organized is your hunting equipment? Do you need to take a Saturday afternoon to come up with a plan for getting all of your gear in order? Further, are you taking proper care of the things that you own? Remember that everything in the heavens and earth belongs to God, so take care of your things with that always in your mind.

PERFECTION

"Every good thing given and every perfect gift is from above, coming down from the Father of lights, with whom there is no variation or shifting shadow."

James 1:17

There are, on occasion, moments afield that approach perfection. These are the times when things come together in such an amazing way that you can't help but lift up your voice in thanks to the Lord for allowing you to experience such things. Times like this may not come often, but when they do it gives you a renewed sense of wonder and awe at what God has created for us to enjoy.

This past April, my buddy Pete and I were turkey hunting down near Lake Wateree here in South Carolina. I had gotten two turkeys in one shot just two days before, and the pressure was off for me for the year. Today I was really hoping that Pete would get his first bird, and I couldn't care less if I saw any turkeys or not.

We started out our hunt by splitting up. I dropped Pete off at one of our logging roads, and then went on down to the same field where I had shot my birds on opening day. I had made myself a little blind by gathering up some dead limbs and branches and bunching them up in front of a tree, and I was nicely hidden within this brush pile when dawn began to break on the horizon.

As the sun peaked through the trees, I heard a turkey fly down behind me, very close. I made some soft yelps on my slate call and was answered with a loud series of the same type of call. Soon a young hen walked into the field, looking left and right trying to find the other hen that she thought she had heard. At one point she stopped a single yard away from my foot, and still she did not see me. It was an incredible moment, but could not compare with what would come later that day.

It wasn't long before the hen left the field, and I sat in silence for a half hour or so as I listened for a turkey to gobble. I heard nothing, but just as I was about to stand up and go get Pete I saw two turkeys way in the distance coming my way down the logging road that my field sat on. They came all the way down the road, but when they got close I could see that they were just Jakes and were not worth shooting.

When they finally left the field, I got up and went to get Pete. He had heard a couple of gobbles, but had not actually seen any turkeys. We decided that we would spend the next couple of hours hunting together, so we drove over to the main logging road on my lease, parked, and then began to slowly walk down the road, stopping every so often to let out a series of yelps and cutts.

After one particularly good series of calls, we got a response from a gobbler that sounded like he was deep down in the swamp below us, maybe three hundred yards or so down into the woods. Grinning at each other, we quickly and quietly slipped into the pines and began to make our way into the swamp. The going was easy since it was downhill, and before long we were deep in the woods. We stopped when we got to the dry creek bed at the bottom of the hill, both of us listening intently.

The gobbler was still calling somewhere in front of us, but as we began to move again a stick cracked in the woods to our left. We both froze, and as we watched a young buck came trotting down the hill in our direction. He was unaware of our presence, and we joyfully watched as he came our way. Behind him was another buck, also young and also ignorant as to the fact that we were standing just a few yards away.

Standing there in the creek bed, our sense of awe increased as both deer stopped on the high bank above us. Standing not ten yards away, the first deer looked me in the eye, but failed to see me for what I was. He began to eat a branch of greenbrier as I whispered to Pete in an almost inaudible voice.

"This is incredible," I said. We were so close to the deer, closer than we would have been had they been in a cage at the zoo. I could see the skin on the back of Pete's neck stretch as he grinned but did not turn to look at me. He remained as still as I was, and the deer remained oblivious to our presence. We stayed this way for several minutes, both of us savoring the moment.

The deer finally moved on, and when they were out of sight Pete turned to me and we again grinned at each other. "That's why we do this," I said to him. "That was one of the most incredible moments that I've ever had in the woods."

Indeed, it had been such a simple thing. Two deer had come our way and had stopped to feed, not knowing that we were there watching. I've been that close to deer in a treestand before, and while camping in a public campground have had a spike buck come right up to me looking for a handout, but this was as close as I had ever been to a wild deer on foot. We both agreed that what we had experienced was something that we would remember for the rest of our lives.

Pete went on to shoot his first turkey later that day, a nice gobbler with a heavy beard and sharp spurs. I went home without a turkey of my own that day, but had seen two deer up close, a hen even closer, and had been with my buddy when he got his first bird. I couldn't have asked for a better day.

Most of us who hunt have lots of good days in the woods. We fill our tags, taking home deer, turkeys and other wild game, but more important than these things are the true gifts from God that we receive when we are afield. Those gifts come not in the form of the taking of game, but in the magical moments of perfection that God gives us from time to time in the deer woods.

ACTION POINT: Watch carefully for those moments in the woods that approach perfection. Recognize them as the gifts from God that they are, and remember to thank Him for each one that you receive.

IN THE COMPANY OF MEN

"Iron sharpens iron, so one man sharpens another."

Proverbs 27:17

I've written before about the need for men to be frequently in the company of other men of like mind; strong in the faith and strong in honor. As political correctness and anti-Christian sentiment both become more and more common in this country, the need to spend time in the company of good men becomes proportionately more important.

Being in the company of men involves much more than just monthly meetings and accountability groups. It means getting involved in each other's lives in such a way that you are willing to speak truth to them even when it is painful. It also means that you have to be open to hearing truths about yourself that you might not want to hear. Further, it means opening up and revealing the deepest hurts and desires within you to the men around you.

About a year or so back I started talking to some of the guys at my church about the need for us to connect with each other on a deeper level. I wanted to see us start "living in community" with each other, praying for each other and doing spiritual battle for each other as the need arose. Four or five men that I talked to had been thinking similar thoughts, and we began to meet on a regular basis. The members of the group have changed slightly over time, but we have now reached a point of stability where a core group of men are committed to getting together every three weeks or so.

We've done several studies together, including Ransomed Heart's *Band of Brothers,* and *Fathered by God.* We've gone through a study on spiritual gifts by Chip Ingram, and we're looking at doing one of David Jeremiah's studies on spiritual warfare. We've also taken turns leading each other through a couple of things without using external media, including taking a look at the armor of God that Paul describes in Ephesians. All of these have been extremely good, and I believe that each of us has grown stronger in our walk with Christ because of the way that we are meeting together and encouraging each other regularly.

The thing that we all keep talking about, however, is the night that I had the guys over to my house for a steak dinner. I bought the best rib-eyes that I could find, and then made my famous baked potatoes to go along with them. I threw together a simple salad, and cooked up a pot of green beans, and then baked some sourdough bread to top it off.

The guys all showed up at my house about the time that the steaks were hitting the grill. We stood on my back deck and took turns shining a spotlight into the woods where we could occasionally see some deer coming into the feeder that I keep out behind my house. We broke bread together with no women around, and had some good, honest conversation about what was going on in our lives.

After the meal, we retreated to the living room where, surrounded by my deer heads, pheasant and duck mounts, we watched a few clips from the movie *Les Miserables.* I showed two scenes chosen to highlight different views of masculinity, and talked about how the transformed Jean Valjean embodied the picture of manhood that we each needed to emulate. His strength when protecting Fantine from the police officer Javert is the same kind of strength that we need to have in our own lives.

Our Bible studies are important; make no mistake. But while we seldom talk about how we had such a great lesson on this night or on that, we do often mention the steak dinner at my house. It's things like this that draw us together as men, and it's this kind of thing that we need to do much more often than we do now to cement the bonds of our friendship.

Most men like guns and weapons, even if they have no experience with them. My buddy Frank once owned an auto parts store down in Gaffney, South Carolina, and after a particularly nasty string of murders occurred in that area he decided that he needed a handgun for protecting the store. He bought a Taurus Judge revolver, and asked me to go with him the first time he shot it. If you're not familiar with it, the Judge shoots both .410 shotgun shells and .45 Long Colt bullets.

We went down to a rifle range in the Sumter National Forest, and we had a great evening shooting his Judge, as well as a few of my rifles. Frank was a quick study, and was soon doing extremely well with his revolver. He also had a blast shooting my AR-15, and the highlight of the evening was when I put a few tracer rounds in the magazine which put on a brilliant light show as dusk began to fall.

I've talked to the guys about going shooting together down there, and I'm still hoping that we can make that happen. There's also a skeet range not far from us up in Gastonia, North Carolina which would be a great place for us to get together and shoot a few rounds. I'm holding out hope that we can do one of these things together before the end of the year.

Regardless of what we end up doing, the point here is that it's vitally important for us to have other men around us to encourage us and to be encouraged in our walks with Christ. Men must do manly things, and these things are best done in the company of like-minded men. Only then can we walk as God commands us to, in the full strength of our masculinity.

ACTION POINT: Do you have men around you who will talk honestly to you about not just their own lives, but also what they see in yours? We need to be men of truth; men who are willing to sharpen and to encourage each other in our Christian walks. This is a critical part of our lives as men.

MORE GOOD EATING

"Every moving thing that is alive shall be food for you; I give all to you, as I [gave] you the green plant."

Genesis 9:3

Although I had only planned to write one entry in this devotional about eating, it is late on a Sunday afternoon in October as I write this, and I have a small Boston Butt out on my smoker that will soon be ready for the table. The smell of the hickory smoke moved me to walk upstairs to my office and write another chapter about food.

It's not so much eating that stirs my heart as it is the act of preparing good food outside, whether it be on a grill, a smoker, or even a simple propane burner. In the last dozen years I've gone through a good many grills and smokers, from small charcoal kettles to my latest acquisition, a Traeger pellet grill. I love them all, and use each of them all year long regardless of the weather.

One of my favorite things to do is to load up my little kettle grill with a bunch of quality charcoal around dusk, get the fire going good, and then sit out on my back deck in the quiet of the evening and watch the coals burn down to a good red glow. Occasionally I can hear deer moving in the woods behind my house, and once or twice I've heard the howl of coyotes as I've sat there in the dark.

I've been known to stand on the back deck and just watch the smoke rise from my Traeger. With a grill like that one, you want to leave it closed to allow the food to cook properly, and so there is no real work involved in it once the meat hits the grill. Nevertheless, I'll poke around in the pellet hopper, or adjust the temperature setting just to give me an excuse to smell the burning hickory or mesquite wood. Even as I write this, I find myself wondering if I need to walk outside and check on my BBQ. I don't, but I can't resist the call of grill.

I keep threatening to buy one of those little backyard fire pits, just so that I'll have another way to sit around a fire here at home. We don't really have a great place to use it; the back deck is made of wood and is attached to the house, so an open fire there would be a bit dangerous. We've got a little swinging bench in the back yard, way down by the woods that would be a decent place for one I guess, and that's probably where I'd end up putting it.

I can easily imagine myself going down there and sitting by the fire on a fall or spring evening, but I can't help but wonder if my wife would take the time to come sit out there with me. I also don't have a good source for firewood, but I guess it would be easy enough to find a downed oak tree somewhere on my deer lease that I could cut into logs and bring home.

I've gotten a little bit off of the subject of food, but campfires have a way of derailing me. Getting back to the topic, another one of my favorite things to do is to deep fry a turkey out in the back yard. I always do this down by my workshop just in case something goes wrong. Turkey fryers are known for erupting in flame, so I do it in an open spot in the yard, keeping a fire extinguisher close at hand. I've yet to have a problem with my fryer, but you do need to be careful with them.

I also love to cook blackened venison tenderloins in my cast iron skillet out on the back deck. I used to use the base of my turkey fryer for a burner, but the ones that come with the frying kits are often pretty poorly made, and I have already lost two of them to exposure to the elements. I finally found a well-built propane burner at an online specialty store, and I had a cover custom made for it that has done quite well at protecting it over the years. Steaks, chicken, and fish also blacken very nicely when I use this method of cooking.

When I'm sitting outside by a fire of any kind, I can't help but feel at great peace with the world around me. It's hard to be stressed when you are tending a fire, or cooking food over a grill of any kind. Times like these are when I find myself conversing with the Lord at the level that comes closest to conversational intimacy. My tendency at these times is not to pray over difficult decisions or to have intercessory prayer for those in need, but rather to have prayer time in which I grow closer to Christ through the peace that an open fire provides.

As a closing note, I'm obliged to tell you that as I wrote this chapter I paused briefly and signed on to the Cabela's website to order myself a backyard fire pit. The act of writing about it stirred me to action, and I'm told that it will arrive in a week or so. That'll be just in time for the cooler weather that is supposed to be heading our way next weekend. I'm looking forward to it.

ACTION POINT: Find some time to sit alone beside a fire of some kind. A campfire or a charcoal grill will do equally well. Take note of the peace of the moment, and use this time to have conversational prayer with God. Make it a habit to do this on a regular basis.

CHOOSING YOUR COMPANIONS WISELY

"He who walks with wise men will be wise, but the companion of fools will suffer harm."

Proverbs 13:20

I have had a number of different hunting companions over the course of my lifetime. Some have been men of like mind as me; many have been strong Christian men who walk with God and know Him well. Others have not been nearly as strong, and in the end I have often had to make the tough choice to stop hunting with some of them.

I've told you before about my neighbor Bobby, and our deer hunting trip to his family's cotton farm that almost ended in disaster when he tried to take a shot at a deer that was frozen in the headlights of my truck. Had he actually have taken the shot, not only could we have been arrested, but under North Carolina law my weapons and even my truck could have been confiscated, and we would have likely been facing some jail time.

I didn't exercise wisdom when I chose to hunt with Bobby. I knew what I was getting into; he was a young man who had not, for the most part, made good choices in his life, and yet this was my first and only chance to hunt on private lands. Going with him to his family farm seemed like the best way for me to actually get that first deer.

Over the years there have been others that I have allowed to hunt with me that I should have shown better wisdom about. In the years after high school, an old classmate named Ernest once called and asked me if I would take him deer hunting with me up to the Uwharrie Game Lands of North Carolina. He had heard about my grandfather's cabin on Badin Lake and how I often used it as a base camp, and he was anxious to get a chance to go deer hunting. He had been small game hunting before, but really wanted to try hunting for something bigger.

I agreed to take him, and one Friday evening we drove up to the cabin together in my truck. As we traveled down the back roads of Montgomery County, I told him how we had to be sure to take good care of the cabin and the things in it, making sure to put everything back in its proper place before we headed back home from the hunt. My grandfather, I told him, was particular about his things, and we needed to be respectful of that.

"It sounds like he's a real jerk," Ernest said.

I was shocked. If that had happened to me today, I would have turned the truck around and taken Ernest back home, regardless of the hour. I'd have driven back to Charlotte, dropped him off at his house, and turned back around again and gone on to the cabin on my own. But at that time in my life I wasn't the person I would later become, and I shrugged off his comment, telling him that it wasn't as bad as he thought.

We went on and hunted together, and although I can't remember if we actually saw anything or not, we definitely didn't get a deer. I do remember that as we pulled off of the dirt road from the game lands and back onto the road that my grandfather's cabin was on, I looked down the road to my right and saw that a couple of game wardens were stopping the other trucks that had been on the game lands.

We turned left, back toward the cabin, and arriving there we gathered our gear and packed the truck to head home. The game wardens were still there at the end of the road when we drove back that way, and they motioned for me to pull the truck over to the side of the road. I complied, and they asked us to step out of the vehicle.

While one of the wardens shined his flashlight in the back of my truck looking for blood, the other asked me why we had turned the other way on the road earlier when we had come out of the woods.

"My grandfather has a house back that way," I told the warden. "We went back there to get our stuff so that we could head back home."

"You didn't shoot a deer and leave it back that way, did you? Do you mind if I search your truck?"

I was an honest hunter then as now, and certainly hadn't done anything wrong. I told the warden that we had indeed not shot anything at all, and that he was welcome to look inside my truck. Together with the other game warden, he looked at our gear and found nothing amiss. The first warden apologized for his attitude toward us, and told me that he had grown suspicious when we turned the other way having seen them stopping vehicles earlier.

Ernest was shaking a little bit when we pulled away from the wardens. I asked him what was wrong, and he pulled his backpack up from the floor of the truck. Opening the zippered pouch on the side, he extracted a little bag of innocent looking mushrooms.

"These," he told me, "are 'shrooms. Psilocybin. I was afraid that they were going to open up my backpack and find them."

The ride home was an extremely quiet one. I didn't yell at Ernest, or blast him in any way. I don't recall whether or not I even spoke to him at all for the rest of the trip home, but I do know for a fact that I never spoke to him again after that incident. I have no doubt that had the wardens found the drugs, Ernest would have let me take the heat for it.

Experiences like this have made it clear to me that we must use good judgment when we decide who we are going to be friends with. We should indeed be witnesses for Christ when we are among the lost, but we should not take them into our close confidence or spend too much time with them. I only regret that I didn't handle either of those situations in a better way.

ACTION POINT: Be extremely particular about the men who you choose to fellowship with. While we have a duty to take the Gospel to the lost, we should spend more time with those who know Christ than with those who don't. The Bible has much to say about this. Take a bit of time to find some other verses that echo this theme.

FRUSTRATION

"Have I not commanded you? Be strong and courageous! Do not tremble or be dismayed, for the LORD your God is with you wherever you go."

Joshua 1:9

When the 2010 deer season began, I faced it with both excitement and trepidation. My wife was pregnant with our first child, and because his due date was in the heart of hunting season I knew that my time afield would be shortened. Each time I went into the woods I was aware that I could receive a phone call from my wife telling me that her time had come, and also that my season would soon come to a swift and yet welcome end.

Although I was extremely happy to be trading at least half of my deer season for the arrival of our child, I had hoped that the first part of the year would be a productive one not from the point of view that I would kill many deer, but that I would both *see* many deer and also use the time afield to mentally prepare for the birth of our child.

It was 97 degrees on the opening day of the season, and I sat roasting in a ground blind for almost twelve hours without seeing a deer. I had two of them blow at me as they approached my stand from different directions, no doubt smelling the sweat that had soaked my clothing, but I never got so much as a look at them. I would have welcomed the sight of the white flag of a retreating deer, but even that was kept from me.

The next two weeks of archery season passed in a similar manner. I spent a half-dozen days afield in one hundred degree weather and never saw a single deer. Each day in the woods was a misery, and yet I would have been even more miserable staying at home knowing that I *could* be out sitting in a deer stand. My frustration at the heat and the lack of deer was growing almost daily. Never before had I gone through a full two weeks of bow season without at least seeing a deer.

When the rifle season opened in mid-September, I put my frustration aside and went to the blind knowing that I would be hot, but that at least I would have a better chance of seeing deer. With my rifle, I could hunt far enough back from the deer that they would not smell the odor of my sweat. I chose a blind that looked productive, and was sitting quietly in it long before daylight on opening morning.

I've already told you earlier in this book how this particular story came out. After sitting in that stand all day, I ended up shooting an eleven point buck. In previous years I had taken a few deer that had more massive antlers than he had, but not by much, and I had never killed one that had more than eight points. The frustration of not seeing deer was broken by the prayer that God answered with that big buck.

The story gets better. Two weeks later I was hunting in a ladder stand on the same section of the lease. My camera had shown me that there were some young bucks still in the area, but I had not seen any that were worth shooting. However, there were a lot of does coming into the area each evening, and since I needed some more meat I decided that I would hunt from this particular stand and try to get a big doe.

By dusk I had still not seen anything. Even with the eleven pointer in the bag, the frustration was again starting to rise. I was beginning to think that this was going to be a one deer year, when as usual, God came through. I saw a deer come out of the woods not thirty yards from my stand. I looked at him through my binoculars and saw that it was a big bodied buck with really tall antlers; much taller than those on my previous deer. I raised my rifle and quickly took the shot.

The buck jumped, obviously hit, and then took off into the woods. There was still a little bit of light, so I stuffed all of my gear into my backpack and then climbed down from the tree and pretty much ran to the spot where the deer had been standing when I had shot him. Blood was easily visible there in the dirt, but more impressive than that was the size of the tracks where the deer had jumped after being shot.

After having worked so hard to retrieve the last buck, I decided to go back down to the sign-in board and wait for some of the other guys to come out of the woods so that I could get some help in tracking this deer. There were already two other fellows there when I arrived, so I quickly recruited them to help me. We raced back up to where I had found the blood.

This time it didn't take very long to find the buck. He was only fifty yards off of the trail, and when we found him I shouted in joy. He was a large eight pointer with a tall rack and massive bases; much bigger than any other whitetail that I've ever taken. He was bigger bodied than the eleven pointer, and looking at him I offered a prayer of thanks to God.

I hunted hard for the next few weeks, still waiting for the birth of our child. In all of that time I only saw two more deer, but having taken two big bucks I could hardly complain about the way the rest of the season might go. It was frustrating to go out time and time again and not see anything, but in the end I'll remember this year as the season of the two big bucks, and not as the season of only seeing a handful of deer.

It's easy to get frustrated in our prayer life and in our daily walk with God as well. So often we feel like our prayers are not being heard, or that they are heard but not answered. Remember that God works in His own time, and if you are praying according to His will and in the name of Jesus, your prayers will be answered. He's promised that to us, and we must trust Him to keep His word.

ACTION POINT: It's easy to get frustrated when you're having an off season. Try to put that aside and just be thankful for any time afield that you are able to get. It's a busy life that we lead, and we should enjoy the time that God provides for us to spend in the woods.

THE PRESSURE IS OFF

"For I am convinced that neither death, nor life, nor angels, nor principalities, nor things present, nor things to come, nor powers, nor height, nor depth, nor any other created thing, will be able to separate us from the love of God, which is in Christ Jesus our Lord."

Romans 8:38-39.

I've been pretty lucky over the course of my many years of deer hunting. As I mentioned before, I killed my first deer back in 1991 after six or seven unproductive years hunting on game lands. I was skunked again in 1992, but I got back on the boards in 1993 when I killed my first buck, which was a fairly good sized spike.

I suffered another setback in 1994 when I again went deerless, but starting in 1995 and continuing on to the present day I've been able to take home at least one deer a year. Indeed, most of the time nowadays I end up shooting five or six deer per season. My wife and I can eat around five deer over the course of the year; the rest I give away to friends who often ask me for venison.

Even now, however, when I have around sixty deer under my belt, I always feel pressure at the beginning of the year to get that first deer out of the way. At my house, we *rely* on a having a good supply of deer meat all year long, and if I don't get at least a couple of deer each year it's a real struggle for us to get along. Now I know we can buy meat at the grocery store, but as most of my readers will be outdoorsmen, I'm sure that they'll understand what I'm talking about.

I'm obviously at my happiest when I can get a deer on the actual opening day of the season. For the last ten years I have kept very detailed records not only about my hunts, but about all of the game that I have taken during my time afield. Surprisingly, since 2000 I have only gotten a deer on two opening days. I wouldn't have thought that, but my records are quite extensive, and that's all that they show.

In 2001 I shot a big doe with my bow and arrow on the opening day of our archery season, and in 2010 I got an eleven point buck on the opening day of general firearms deer season. My worst season of all, not counting all of the years where I was completely skunked, was back in 2004 when I only got one deer; a spike buck on the first of December, over two months into the deer season.

Most of the hunters that I talk to express similar feelings about killing a deer early in the year. "The pressure is off," my friends will say to me after they fill their first tag of the year. I know the feeling well, and it is a wonderful thing to be able to relax for the rest of the year.

Now, as I said, I do keep detailed records not only of my hunts, but also of the animals that I kill. It's not that it's a numbers game; I just like looking back on the list and picking out a hunt to sit and remember on miserable days in February or March, when all of the hunting seasons are closed. And like most hunters, it's not the kill that determines the success of a hunt for me, but I'd be lying if I said it wasn't important to me to get at least one deer per year.

I do love the feeling of knowing, once that first deer is down, that the season will again end with venison in the freezer. I love it when the pressure is off for the year. In that miserable year of 2004, I was indeed feeling quite discouraged by the time that December came around. I just wasn't even *seeing* deer that year, and so although I'd already taken a dozen bucks in the years leading up to 2004, even that little spike was a trophy to me on that cold December day.

Even more importantly, it's wonderful to know that the pressure is *really* off once we've truly accepted Christ into our hearts. We're still called to be holy, and yet we can at least be assured that our salvation is secure and that nothing can take that away. This is a topic, I'm sure, that will be controversial among my brothers of different denominations.

I'll lay claim to being a Southern Baptist, and we believe in the doctrine of eternal salvation. "Once saved, always saved" is what we believe the Bible teaches, and verses such as the one that is included at the top of this chapter confirm this belief. Many men of different denominations that I've talked to feel otherwise, but I've never had one of them convince me that this doctrine is wrong.

I've also heard men talk about us, being saved, no longer being under the Law and thus being free to do whatever we want. Indeed, if you are truly saved then you are *not* under the law, but you still have a duty to live a holy life. These men base their belief on Paul's statement that "all things are lawful for me," but they often leave out the second half of that verse which says "but not all things are profitable."

My goal in this book is not to convince you to see things as I do, but rather to toss out topics that I hope will trigger you to think about these issues in a deep manner. For me, I will be content in knowing that I am indeed eternally secure in my salvation, and I will continue to strive to live a life that honors Christ. I'll fail often, as history has shown, but at least I'll do it knowing that the pressure is off.

ACTION POINT: Think about the doctrine of eternal salvation. If you, like me, believe that this is what the Bible teaches, are you able to clearly state why you believe this? If you don't believe it, would you be willing to take on a personal Bible study to look deeper into this matter?

THE ROCKS CRY OUT

"Some of the Pharisees in the crowd said to him, 'Teacher, rebuke Your disciples.' But Jesus answered, 'I tell you, if these become silent, the stones will cry out!'"

Luke 19:39-40

I love to hunt, but it is not just the hunting itself that I am drawn to. What I really love is being in the wild places of the world and experiencing creation outside of the boundaries of the cities and other populated areas of the country. There are stands on my deer lease that I hunt from more frequently than others simply because they are so rugged and trigger some longing for adventure deep inside of me.

Indeed, some of the moments afield that mean the most to me are those times before getting in the stand early in the morning, when the starts are still shining high in the sky, and those last few minutes in the stand before I have to leave for home. I will often stretch these moments out for as long as possible, savoring them like a fine wine.

There is one particular stand on my lease that is very unusual for this part of the country. There is an old dirt pit off to one side of our property that has been cut out of a mountain, and there is a sheer cliff that is at least 75 feet high that overlooks this pit. Perched on the edge of the cliff is a box blind, and sitting in that you can see far down into the swamps below.

I usually hunt this stand in the mornings, and it's an amazing place to be when the sun starts to rise. To the left I can see the shores of Lake Watcrce, and can often watch the fishing boats as they head out in search of bass and crappie. Far in front of me a road winds its way along the lakeshore, and to my right I see the edge of one of the many swamps that cover our lease.

I have watched in awe as a beautiful red fox climbed straight up the cliff wall not twenty yards from the stand, and I have seen a bald eagle perched high in a tree that sits not much farther away. I've seen deer moving in the old dirt pit below me, and have watched coyotes cross the road way up as far away as I can see.

When I leave that blind each morning, I often stand as close to the edge of the cliff as I dare and just look out over the world. It's a great place to take in the majesty of creation, and I especially love standing there on grey October days when the leaves are brilliant with the changing colors and the wind is whispering in the pines around me. I can't help but feel connected to God when I'm standing in this place.

I am always reluctant to pull away from that particular place, and it is with slow steps that I turn and walk away when it's finally time to go. No other place on my lease moves me like that one does, although there are many other places in the wide world where I have felt that way. The shores of Cape Point on the Outer Banks of North Carolina stir similar feelings in me, and there's an old field deep in the woods of the Uwharrie Game Lands that I am drawn to year after year.

I'm thankful that I have so many beautiful places that I can go where I can look around me and see what God has wrought. In cities I see the hand of man, and I am not impressed. It's in the wild, untouched places that I feel the closest to God, and it is to those places that I'll return over and over and stand in wonder as I look at what He has made.

ACTION POINT: Even if we did not have the Word of God, we would be able to see evidence of Him in the world around us. His work cries out to Him in worship, and you can easily see this whenever you stop to look upon the beauty of the rivers, fields, and forests of our country. Make an effort to look for the work of His hand the next time you are afield.

FIGHTING FOR THIS DEVOTIONAL

"But the prince of the kingdom of Persia was withstanding me for twenty-one days; then behold, Michael, one of the chief princes, came to help me, for I had been left there with the kings of Persia."

Daniel 10:13

Writing this devotional has been an incredible struggle for me on both a spiritual and a physical level. I have published two books prior to this one, and neither of those efforts was attacked, and yet this book, because it deals with God, has been under constant attack from the very beginning. Spiritual warfare is a very real thing; the battle that we as believers are fighting is likewise a very real one.

When I'm not writing books or hunting deer, I work as a computer programmer for a large, well known corporation. I've been with them for almost twenty years now, and am extremely happy with my job. But it was at my job that the spiritual attacks that I faced during the course of writing this book were at their worst.

Being a programmer now, and before that a mainframe database administrator, I am extremely familiar with long hours and pagers going off in the middle of the night, calling on me to solve problems in our production environments. But in the months that have passed since I started writing this book, I have been under constant stress at work. My days often go beyond the ten hour mark, with work starting at 6:00am and often not finishing until close to 6:00pm.

I've had more days when meetings have interfered with my lunch hour than ever, and seldom have I hung up my hat at the time that I had previously become accustomed to finishing up work for the day. As I said, my job is a good one and I am happy to be working for this company, but the stress has been almost unbearable. This almost certainly has its origin in the spiritual world, although I'm sure some of you may find that hard to swallow.

On top of that, I've written many times about the baby that my wife and I are expecting. As I write this, we are only about three weeks away from his birth, and though we've worked hard to get the house ready for him, there is still much that needs to be done. The other half of the attack on me comes in at this level.

Almost exactly when things at work picked up steam, my wife and I entered a period of activity of after-hours errands like I have never seen before in my life. In the last three months, I've had exactly two days where I could finish work and then just sit down and relax for a bit. Two days, and that is not an exaggeration. If it's not a doctor's appointment, it's a trip to the baby store. I've even had to ask Frank, a close friend with whom I meet on a weekly basis to study the Word with, to take a break for a few months.

My Bible reading has suffered, my prayer life has suffered, and I'm sure my health has suffered as well. A couple of routine blood pressure checks at my doctor's office have shown this to be true. I'm typically a fairly stress-free person, and this part of my life is another place where the Enemy has chosen to attack me. More than anything else though, it seems that every effort that I've made to sit down and do a bit of writing on this devotional has been thwarted.

There have been many days when I have had to insist on setting absolutely everything aside – including church – just so that I could get a little bit of work done on the book. For many years I've felt the call to work with sportsmen in some manner fitting of the Lord, and I really believe that this book is the first step in that process. I believe that God wanted me to write this book not only for you, but for me as well, for my own spiritual growth. With a baby on the way, I had to work hard to get the book finished, knowing that once he arrives my time will be even more limited.

Even the first half of this year's deer season has been stressful. The entire month of September brought one-hundred degree temperatures to our area, and not a single moment that I spent in a stand was comfortable. Couple that with the fact that I haven't been seeing deer this year and you end up with one frustrated hunter. I'm thankful though that out of the three deer that I've seen this season, two of those were the best bucks that I've ever taken in my life, so even in my stress, God provided for me.

In those months, He has also kept me well-supplied with things to write about. I have not lacked for ideas, and often I would keep a notebook at hand just so that I could write down anything that popped into my head when I was away from my desk. He has also taught me how to better handle stress when it does come my way. Being a fairly laid-back man, I haven't always been good at dealing when stress when it occurs.

But now the cooler weather is here, and the days that I am spending afield are much more tolerable than what I was previously enduring. I've got a bunch of time off from work coming up, and I'm hoping that it will refresh me and help me recover strength for the next big wave of long hours that I am facing. And our child is almost here; just seeing his face will be an event of great joy.

Keep in mind what I said earlier. The battle is real. Things like this book are heavily opposed by our Enemy. Satan will do everything he can to cause me to put down my pen, so to speak, just as he will attack you in anything that you do for the Lord. We must be prepared to do battle with him; we must be familiar with the Armor of God so that we can turn him away in Christ's name.

I feel like I've complained a lot in this chapter, but I really wanted you to get some idea of how real this spiritual battle has been. I am typically not one to talk about my misery or complain about my situation, but in this case the attacks have been so obvious that it is almost comical. I felt like I had to write at least a little bit about it.

Although writing this book has been an incredible fight for me, I will not stop. I have had many friends praying for me as I sit at my desk and write, and though this book is something that won't even be remembered in ten years, nor counted among the great Christian works of our time, it is what I have been called to write, and I have answered that call. I have fought the good fight, and am almost finished with this particular race. I have kept the faith.

> **ACTION POINT:** Spiritual warfare is something that you will face more and more as you grow in your relationship with God. The Enemy will do everything that he can to damage that relationship. Learn how to do battle at the spiritual level. Go forth to victory and celebrate, for Christ has already won.

SHED HUNTING

"As to this salvation, the prophets who prophesied of the grace that [would come] to you made careful searches and inquiries, seeking to know what person or time the Spirit of Christ within them was indicating as He predicted the sufferings of Christ and the glories to follow."

1 Peter 1:10-12

When deer season comes to an end each year, I often feel a great sense of loss in my life. Hunting is my favorite activity; I'm not a big sports fan, I do not watch much television, and I don't go to parties and bars. For four months of the year, I go afield as often as possible, and when that time comes to an end I usually don't know what to do with myself.

I do a bit of duck hunting in January and early February, and will go predator hunting once in a while as well, but those things only feel like a shadow of what deer hunting is to me. Around the first of March though, my spirits lift a little bit because it's time to start looking for shed deer antlers. I'd rather hunt for sheds than for ducks or coyotes, and finding a good antler is more rewarding to me than shooting a duck or predator.

On a late winter day, I'll strike out for my deer lease wearing heavy overalls, since when I shed hunt I go deep into the briar-filled swamps on my search for antlers. I wear a backpack that starts out empty, since this is what I'll use to carry any sheds that I find. I also go heavily armed; I usually take one of my AR-15 rifles along with me as they are light enough to carry all day but powerful enough to discourage anything that I run into, be it wild boar or black bear.

I like to cover many miles of swampland on each of these hunts, searching every briar patch carefully and moving very slowly, inspecting every inch of ground as I look for antlers. I have had great luck in finding entire deer skulls with both antlers intact; the workbench in my garage has four nice ones on display that I've found over the years, but only rarely do I find a shed antler.

Last year I spent six hours searching one particular swamp bottom where many bucks had been seen during the season. I started off my hunt by taking careful note of an old pine tree that was marked with a splash of blue paint on its trunk. It was just across the creek from where I would be starting, and I knew that I would recognize it when I came back to it.

I made a huge loop through the woods, cutting a trail through the briars with my clippers and inspecting every likely spot that might hold the object of my quest. I found nothing, and even in the cold winter air I was sweating freely as I made my way from one end of the swamp to the other.

Walking in a wide loop that followed the natural curve of the creek bottom, I finally saw the blue-painted pine tree ahead of me in the distance. I had walked for miles and found nothing, but as I arrived at my landmark I looked down and saw a beautiful chocolate colored antler lying on the ground at the base of the tree. I almost wept a bit when I picked it up. I had looked so hard, had done this so many times, and had finally found an antler that looked like it could have been dropped that very morning.

I had found many old, squirrel-chewed antlers over the years, but never before had I come across one that had only recently fallen from the head of the buck that bore it. The irony of the fact that I found it not ten yards from where I started my search was not lost on me, but neither did I begrudge myself the time spent deep in the woods. The time had been good for me, and though I was physically exhausted, I was mentally recharged.

I had been looking for more than just antlers, you see. I was trying to reconnect with God on a conversational level; and I had been praying aloud as I walked through the swamp. I was not praying for anything specific, although I'm sure I mentioned to God a time or two that it would be nice if He would throw an antler my way. More than anything else, I was enjoying the uninhibited conversational prayer that the solitude of the swamp allowed. I was enjoying being able to freely speak to God without worrying that someone might hear what I was saying.

As I think about how hard I've worked searching for shed antlers over the years, I can't help but compare that to how hard some people search fruitlessly for God in all of the wrong ways. I think about things like the prosperity gospel, and the modern "seeker" movement, all of whom are looking for a version of God that they are not going to find.

It saddens me sometimes to see people searching for God in the things of the world when He has already spoken to us very clearly in both the Bible and through His Son Jesus. If they would search the Word for what they are looking for as diligently as I search the woods for antlers, they might find what they seek.

ACTION POINT: Searching for antlers is a great way to reconnect with the deer season months after it has ended. It's also a great way to introduce a child to the outdoors, as you can do this together with children who are too young to hunt. Use this time to also reconnect with God, and when searching for Him, look to His Word, not to the things of the world.

PROMOTING HUNTING

"I solemnly charge [you] in the presence of God and of Christ Jesus, who is to judge the living and the dead, and by His appearing and His kingdom: preach the word; be ready in season [and] out of season; reprove, rebuke, exhort, with great patience and instruction."

2 Timothy 4:1-2

As you are well aware, hunting is a controversial activity. Many people are turned off by the thought of killing animals; others are against our sport because they have been influenced by the media and by public perception and are afraid of guns. Hunting, they say, is a barbaric activity that has no place in the modern world. We've all likely encountered people who have this kind of negative view of hunting.

In the chapter *The Dominion of Man*, I talked about the relatively small number of times that I have had to deal with anti-hunters over the course of my hunting life. From time to time I still come across people who are against what we do, but to a person they are only able to base their view on the way that they have seen hunting portrayed on various television shows and in movies. Their arguments against us have no real basis in fact, and thus when confronted with the truth their opinion can often be swayed.

When I first booked my African safari in 2006, one of the things that surprised me the most was how interested people were in the trip. I got the chance to talk about how safari hunting has been the salvation of African wildlife, and my listeners were amazingly receptive to what I had to say. People of all ages and backgrounds asked wonderfully intelligent questions about the trip, and in the end not one of them had anything negative to say to me about my plans. It was truly a great experience.

Fred Bear, one of the fathers of modern bowhunting, often told young Ted Nugent that he should always promote hunting, but never defend it. I've been fortunate enough to meet Mr. Nugent on several occasions, and have heard him talk about this tactic many times. It's a brilliant strategy, and I believe that each of us who hunts has a duty to become as informed as possible about the facts when it comes to hunting and conservation. With the right information at our disposal, we cannot be overcome.

The biggest thing that we have going for us in this battle is that we are on the right side. It's a proven fact that regulated hunting and good, common sense game management is one of the key factors in the success of the conservation of wildlife. The wild turkey is a great example of this. No other species has made such a dramatic comeback as the turkey. Where once it was almost unheard of to see or hear a turkey, twice now in the last year I have seen them in urban areas where you would not have thought that they could survive.

Most hunters can tell you that there are more deer in America today than there were when the pilgrims arrived in our country many centuries ago. Indeed, most game animals are thriving, and it's completely due to the good game management practices that have been implemented in most of the states in this country. And non-game animals like the condor remain in jeopardy to this day.

I wonder, though, how many of you hunters and outdoorsmen would know what I mean when I mention the Pittman-Robertson Act. If you're not familiar with what this is, then this is your starting point for arming yourself with information when it comes to promoting (and not defending) hunting. For those who don't know what this is, I'll take a few minutes to explain it.

In 1937, at the request and the urging of sportsmen, Congress passed a law that placed an excise tax on the purchase of guns and ammunition. The funds from this tax were then sent back to the states for use in financing wildlife conservation and restoration projects across the country. The result was that many species of both game and non-game animals began to thrive and recover from the devastating losses that they had previously suffered not only at the hands of unregulated market hunting but also due to loss of habitat as the country became urbanized.

This tax is still in effect today, and it is financed not only by the purchase of guns and ammunition, but also by the purchase of any kind of archery equipment. One estimate that I have seen states that sportsmen contribute 3.5 million dollars *per day* to this fund. Keep in mind that this tax is not something that was thrust upon us. The sportsmen of the early Twentieth Century were foresighted enough to see the benefit of it, and they *asked* for and received this tax.

Armed with this information as a starting point, you can now begin to intelligently discuss at least one way in which hunters have strongly contributed to the restoration and conservation of both game and non-game animals. There are many other ways in which we exercise our stewardship over the environment, but start here, and start promoting hunting when you talk to people about it.

One of the key factors for *not* defending hunting is that to defend it, there must be at least some preconception that it *might* be wrong. Since real science shows that it is indeed good for the survival of wildlife, we must never even acknowledge for a minute that the anti-hunters might have a point. They don't. The only basis that they have is *feelings*. Feelings that the animals suffer pain when they are shot; feelings that the killing of animals is a barbaric practice.

You know what? It *does* hurt an animal when it's shot. But what animal ever really dies a pleasant death in a nice bed surrounded by its loved ones? The reality is that animals kill and eat each other every day, and most animals are alive when the eating process begins. Better to suffer briefly from a bullet or an arrow than to lie on the ground and watch as some carnivore starts to devour you.

One of the things I've struggled with quite often is the question of how do I apply this concept to my Christianity? Apologetics is an interesting area of Christianity, and yet its entire approach is to defend our faith. Some of the best minds in the Christian world today are our apologists, with great thinkers like Ravi Zacharias, Dinesh D'Souza, and Lee Strobel defending Christianity on a daily basis. How then can I criticize the concept of defending something that you wholly believe in? I'm struggling with this one, my friends.

One of the guys in my "band of brothers" is greatly interested in apologetics, and I share his passion for getting into the nuts and bolts of the faith and learning about the martyrs who have suffered for Christianity over the years. When the apostles were put to death one by one, you know that they *had* to have a solid belief in what it was that they were dying for. That alone should be enough to convince people that Christ was and is who He said He was, and yet for many people it is not.

I'll continue to think about this topic, and will ultimately reconcile my belief that we should promote hunting rather than defend it with my love of Christian apologetics. These two viewpoints do not have to be in agreement for me to have a consistent worldview, but I think it would help if they were.

ACTION POINT: Learn how to promote hunting. Educate yourself in the many ways that hunting benefits wildlife as a whole. Likewise, educate yourself in the Bible and in matters that are important to Christianity. Be ready at all times to explain why you believe what you believe.

FUTURE GENERATIONS

"These words, which I am commanding you today, shall be on your heart. You shall teach them diligently to your sons, and shall talk of them when you sit in your house, and when you walk by the way and when you lie down, and when you rise up."

Deuteronomy 6:6-7

I went on my first deer hunt back in 1985. I had grown up hunting doves and squirrels in the woods and fields that bordered our south Charlotte neighborhood, but I didn't get a real chance to go after deer until I was home from college for the Christmas break from my freshman year. A neighbor of mine invited me and another friend along for an afternoon hunt down in Weddington, NC on the day after Christmas.

We saw no deer that day, but I was quickly hooked on hunting them. It wasn't until I transferred from Montreat-Anderson College down to the University of North Carolina at Charlotte that I really got a chance to start seriously deer hunting. I've told you before about how I spent the last part of my college career hunting on the Uwharrie Game Lands, and how shortly after that I got a chance to chase deer on private lands when my dad set up a hunt for me on his friend Arnold's property.

Over the next few years, Arnold taught me quite a bit about deer hunting, and before long I had become pretty successful at it, bringing home several deer each year. It's been fifteen years now since I got skunked during the course of a hunting season, and I credit that to the lessons that I learned during those many years of hunting with Arnold.

In more recent years, I've been able to take my friend Pete hunting with me and help him get not only his first fox, but also his first deer and turkey. It's been a joy watching him evolve as a hunter, and I hope to see him pass his love of the sport on to his grandchildren. Pete and I are the same age, and though it's been fun teaching him about deer, I've often wished that I had someone a good bit younger than me to take along with me in the deer woods.

More than once the thought has come to me that it would be nice if one of my non-hunting friends had a son who was interested in hunting so that I could take him along and teach him to hunt deer, much like Arnold taught me. The ability to hunt well is a skill that can be learned when you are on your own, but it's much better when you are with someone who can pass on information about deer behavior, tracks, and sign.

Indeed, the number of hunters that go afield each year has been on the decline as the urbanization of America continues. With that in mind, it is up to us to pass on this legacy to our children and grandchildren. We must teach our children the benefit that hunting provides to wildlife, but beyond that we need to pass on the love for the land itself that most hunters feel. If we could teach our young people to put a high value on the woods and fields of our country, the desire to hunt in them will not be far behind. We must talk about these things with the next generation.

Scripture likewise instructs us to talk about the things of God constantly with our children. We are told that we should bring Him up in our conversations at all times, so that our children will come to know Him like we do. I believe that it is important that we follow through on this and pass on the most important legacy of all to them. As important as hunting is for future generations to enjoy, a life in Christ is infinitely more valuable.

ACTION POINT: Pass on the traditions of hunting and fishing to your children. If you don't have kids, perhaps you have coworkers whose children might enjoy learning to hunt. Learn to talk about the benefits of hunting and of time spent afield. Likewise, talk often about the things of God, not only to your children, but to everyone around you.

LOST!

"'I will feed My flock and I will lead them to rest,' declares the Lord God. 'I will seek the lost, bring back the scattered, bind up the broken and strengthen the sick; but the fat and the strong I will destroy. I will feed them with judgment.'"

Ezekiel 34: 15-16

Although I have spent a great many hours and days afield, I've only actually gotten lost once, and in that case I was really only temporarily turned around and soon found my way back to camp. Two other times I've been present when others have lost their way, but each of those cases were also quickly set right.

Many years ago I was deer hunting on my friend Arnold's property. I had chosen to spend the afternoon in a fairly new stand that I had never been to before, and although the trail to the stand was marked with little reflective tacks that had been pushed into the bark of the trees, whoever had marked the trail had only put them on one side of each tree. The result was that you could find your way to the stand in the morning, but they did not show you the way out in the evening.

The stand wasn't even that deep in the woods once you left the main trail. It couldn't have been more than one hundred yards from the logging road, but the leaves were still heavy on the trees on the day that I chose to hunt from that particular stand. I remember that I found my way in just fine, and was soon settled comfortably in the tree waiting for deer. I also remember that a few deer came into the area to feed on white oak acorns, but that none of them were big enough to shoot.

I've always been one for staying in the stand until the last possible moment, so it would have been a little bit after dark when I finally climbed back down. I got out my flashlight, shouldered my backpack and began to walk back toward the main road. Because there were no reflective tacks on my side of the trees, I had to occasionally turn around and shine my light back in the direction that I had come so that I could be sure that I was still on the trail.

To my dismay, my flashlight quickly started to go dim as the batteries began to die. Before long it was not putting out enough light to illuminate the trail markers behind me, and it certainly wasn't doing me any good looking forward. Within minutes, I was standing in the dark with only the light of the moon to guide my way.

I continued on in a straight line, figuring that I would soon come to the road. The good news was that Arnold's tract of land was only 160 acres, so if I traveled far enough in a single direction I would come to a road before too long. Though I did not know it, I had started to bear off in the wrong direction and was heading slightly away from the road that I had come in on. Although I must have been quite close to that road, I began to get a bit worried as I walked and walked but never came out on it.

After about 15 minutes I stopped and listened. There was no sound of human activity to be heard; only the call of night birds, owls, and crickets. I then did exactly what I knew better than to do. Rather than staying put and waiting for Arnold to come looking for me, I struck off again, this time in a slightly panicked walk-run, and again not knowing it I headed deeper and deeper into the woods on the back side of his property.

I walked for a half hour, and eventually came to a deep creek that I did not recognize, though in later years would know it well as I leased the land that surrounded it. As I stood looking at the creek, I heard a vehicle off to my right, and was surprised to see headlights come around a bend in the little dirt road that bordered Arnold's property. I was not twenty yards from that road, and when the truck passed I walked out of the woods and knew where I was.

I was almost a mile and a half (by the main road) from Arnold's little trailer, and was probably a quarter mile from the back gate where the road that I *should* have come out on was. Sighing with relief, and yet feeling stupid, I hitched my backpack up higher on my shoulders and began hiking up the road to the back gate.

Once at the gate, I still had to walk a long way from there to the camp without the benefit of a flashlight. I was sweating freely and still feeling stupid when I got back to the trailer and found Arnold and a few other guys waiting for me. Arnold ventured a guess that I had stayed so late in the woods because I must have had deer around my stand and not wanted to scare them off when I climbed down. Being embarrassed about getting lost, I told him that he had guessed correctly. It wasn't until several years later that I came clean about getting lost in his woods.

I mentioned two other times where I had been involved when other people had gotten turned around in the woods. Once, on a hunt up in the Uwharrie Game Lands in North Carolina, one of the fellows that went with me got a bit lost in a situation similar to the one that I just described. It had been snowing that day, and we had parked my truck at the base of a mountain and had each gone in different directions for our afternoon hunt.

As evening fell, I made my way back down the mountain to my truck. I figured that my friend would soon be along, but twenty minutes later he had still not shown up. I started getting a bit worried and called for him several times, even honking the horn of my truck once or twice. When he failed to answer, I waited fifteen more minutes and then fired a series of three shots into a dirt bank on the side of the road.

Ten minutes after that, my friend arrived back at my truck, shaking his head. Being unfamiliar with the country, he had indeed found his way down the mountain, but had turned the wrong way when he came to the road. He was walking away from the truck instead of toward it, and upon hearing my shots he had realized this and had turned around and started moving in the right direction.

The third and most comical episode of getting lost happened when I was on a gemsbok hunt in Africa. After taking a shot at one of these big antelope through a thicket of briars and watching it run off, the professional hunter, the native tracker, and myself had found a couple of spots of blood where the animal had been standing. Zwei, the professional hunter, had decided to search in one direction, sending me and my tracker, Jacob, off in another.

We spread out with Zwei ranging far ahead, me in the middle, and Jacob moving off to the east. The little tracking dog that was with us was running freely, and once in a while I would stop to listen to see if I could hear him bark. We moved further and further apart, each going deeper into the bush. I paused and listened to the silence, amazed at how quiet everything was. Jacob and Zwei were nowhere in sight.

Although I was concerned about the minimal amount of blood that we were finding, I took some time to savor the moment. It was wonderful to be standing alone in Africa, in thick brush. As I stood contemplating the situation, a warthog came tearing by me at high speed, and I laughed with joy as I watched him go.

Before long I moved on, still trying to find some sign in the dry dirt. I heard a whistle off to my right, and paused. It came again: definitely human. I whistled back and began walking in that direction. I had walked a long distance, longer than I would have thought, before I heard the whistle again, this time just yards away. I stepped out of the thicket and found Jacob waiting for me. "You must come with me now," he said in his thickly accented baritone.

I followed, hoping that they had found my gemsbok. Jacob didn't say anything else for a while; he just walked, and I walked along behind him. I know we walked for at least a mile and a half when he finally turned to me, sheepish, and said, "I look for de *bakkie*." The truck. He couldn't find the truck. My tracker was lost.

I shook my head, at least inwardly, and laughed. The truck was back in the other direction, over a mile from where we were now. He hadn't told me where we were going, or I would have set him straight earlier on. I was about to tell him where the truck was when the radio buzzed. Zwei was calling. I couldn't follow the conversation in Afrikaans, but I did hear the word "bakkie" several times and "dumb" at least twice. Zwei was not happy that Jacob could not find the truck. He told Jacob where it was, and then signed off.

"Wait here," said Jacob. All too happy to oblige, I sat down in the shade on the side of the road and watched him jog off back toward where we had parked. He was gone for a half hour or so, and as I wandered around the little area I was waiting in I found a porcupine quill lying in the red dirt of the road. I picked it up, the first of several that I would find and bring home hidden deeply in the bottom of my luggage.

Jacob finally arrived with the truck, and once I was aboard we drove over to where Zwei was waiting for us with the tracking dog. We never did find that gemsbok, but at least my tracker found his way back to the truck. He took a good bit of ribbing, especially when the guys back in camp found out that I had known where the truck was the whole time and just hadn't realized what it was that Jacob was looking for.

Being lost isn't always funny. In the examples that I gave, there was never any real danger. In all three cases, there was no chance that anyone would have had to spend the night in the wild, or have a search party sent out to look for them. This isn't always the case. For those that don't know Christ, being lost is a matter that has eternal consequences. We who do know Him have the Holy Spirit to guide us and to encourage us, but this is not the case for everyone.

ACTION POINT: Getting lost in the woods is not much fun. With modern tools such as the GPS, it's not very easy to get lost, but if you're afield in unfamiliar territory and get turned around, remember that the first action to take is to stay put, stay calm, and think about your situation. If you are spiritually lost, let Christ be your compass.

LAST LIGHT

"Who stills the roaring of the seas; the roaring of their waves, and the tumult of the peoples. They who dwell in the ends [of the earth] stand in awe of Your signs; You make the dawn and the sunset shout for joy."

Psalm 65:7-8

As the sun begins to set behind the trees on the last day of deer season, I sit in my stand for a few extra minutes to stop and reflect on the year and the way that it has gone. A plentitude of new memories have been made, and another season has passed in which the Lord has greatly blessed my time afield. There are new trophies to hang on my walls, and plenty of meat to enjoy in the coming months.

I have spent numerous hours in the woods over the course of the season, and have watched the sun rise and set more times than I can count. I almost always get depressed when deer season comes to an end, but this year I'm not feeling it quite as much. When I was younger, it seemed like it took forever for the hunting seasons to arrive, but now that I've reached middle-age I know that next year's opening day will come long before I am really ready for it.

And I've got my new son to think about. Born in the heart of this year's season, there will be so many things to do with him that I'm sure the time will fly by between now and next September. And in the years after that, I'll look forward to taking him into the woods with me, and will hope that he chooses to be a sportsman like me. Only time will tell, but I'll do everything that I can to encourage him to come to love the outdoors the way that I do.

There are also likely to be many changes at our lease next year. The loggers have come and gone, and we've got a lot of work to do. We'll need to reposition our current permanent stands to take advantage of the new clear cuts and shooting lanes, and all of our fields will need to be reworked to get them in shape for next season.

We're also talking about putting tougher restrictions on our bucks in an effort to get better quality antler growth out of them. We're talking about leaving all of the deer that are younger than five years old alone, and only taking bucks once they have reached full maturity. This will cause a lot of debate among the members of the club, and we'll ultimately all need to reach an agreement as to how we want to handle this.

Whatever changes come our way, we'll be sure to remember that God is in control of it all. He has made this beautiful land for us to hunt on, and He also made the very deer that we hunt. I will continue to stand in awe of His creation, and will look forward to the next time that I step out into the wilderness with a gun on my shoulder and a pack on my back. And I will continue to be thankful to Him for creating me to be a sportsman.

ACTION POINT: As deer season comes to a close, take some time to reflect on what you've seen in the woods this year. Every sunrise and every sunset is a blessing from God, and we are privileged to be able to see them from the unique perspective of living the sportsman's way of life. Be sure to thank God for the season that you've had, and ask Him to bless each and every one of your future hunts.

AFTERWORD

It took me a bit longer than I originally planned to write this book. One of the interesting things though is that I never once ran out of things to write about. When I sat down to start writing the book, I made a list of possible topics and saved them in a little text file on my computer. There were a dozen topics in the document, and as I finished writing about each one I would delete it from the file.

The interesting part is that for the six months that it took me to write this book, there were *always* ten or twelve ideas still to be written about in that little file. I would be driving to my deer lease, running errands, or talking with a buddy when an idea would come to me. I'd make a note of it and add it to the file at the first chance that I got to do so. As soon as I got a chapter written, another idea would pop into my head.

My hesitation in writing the book had been that I wouldn't come up with enough things to write about, or that there wouldn't be enough variety in the topics that I chose for the book. I think God was speaking to me, keeping me supplied with a constant stream of ideas, and in the end there was more than enough material to fill the book. In fact, even though the book is done there are *still* a half dozen ideas or so left to write about. I'm hoping that this book does well enough to warrant a second volume to use them in.

My real hope, though, is that you've gotten something out of this book. I hope that it has encouraged you in your Christian walk and that in some small way it will help to bring you closer to God. It's been a huge learning experience for me, and my own walk has been strengthened as I struggled to get the book finished. The chapter called *Fighting for this Devotional* only told part of the story; it was indeed a battle to find time to complete this work, and I as I write this afterword I can hardly believe that it is indeed finally finished.

There are more books to come in the *Hunting for the Heart of God* series, and I hope also that you'll stick around and see what's next. There will likely be another devotional, and ultimately I hope to write a full book that again encourages men to live *as* men, all while keeping with the theme of hunting and the outdoors.

As always, if you have any questions or comments, I'd be happy to answer your email. Get in touch with me at sean@seanjeffries.com. It may take me a bit of time to respond, but I'll do my best to answer as quickly as possible.

Sean Jeffries
Clover, South Carolina

October 2010

ABOUT THE AUTHOR

Sean Jeffries is a life-long hunter who has a passion for sharing his experiences afield with others. He has kept detailed journals of every hunt that he has undertaken since 2000, and is the owner and operator of the Wingshooters.net website. He has a heart for men's ministry, with a strong focus on sportsmen.

His books include "Eight Days in Africa" and "A Life Spent Afield". Sean's next work will continue the *Hunting for the Heart of God* collection, and will be available in mid-2011. He also plans a second devotional which will be in the same format as the one in which you have just read.

Sean lives in Clover, SC with his wife Micki, their two dogs, and their soon-to-be-born son Paul.

Deer Hunter's Devotional

CPSIA information can be obtained at www.ICGtesting.com
Printed in the USA
LVOW060029311212

313819LV00002B/115/P